Leadership 2.0

Leading Successful Teams, Businesses, Communications and Decisions Based on Neuroscience, Social Psychology and Leadership Principles

Peter Allen

Premium Content

Subscribe to our receive premium content on productive meetings, business success, marketing mastery, sales conversion, team management and much more

https://www.subscribepage.com/premiumcontent

Access

Table of Contents

Introduction

"Leadership is simply causing other people to do what the leaders want. Good leadership, whether formal or informal, is helping other people rise to their full potential while accomplishing the mission and goals of the organization. All members of an organization, who are responsible for the work of others, have the potential to be good leaders if properly developed."

~ Bob Mason

Imagine a large, multinational corporation has just hired you as their new sales and marketing director in their international sales division. Global sales have been on a downward trend for several months, and you've been given what seems to be the impossible task of pulling an entire division back on track. You've hardly been given any information on your predecessor, your team, or your peers within the organization. All you know for sure is that there's a six-month window for you to prove yourself and implement positive change within the division. While six months sounds like enough time, you know you'll have to pull out all the stops if there's any hope of making it work.

Just then, the first signs of doubt and despair enter your mind. How are you going to succeed in turning an entire division around when you're not even sure what different types of personalities with which you're going to be working? You've already heard some water cooler gossip that staff is placing side bets on how long you're likely to last before you crack. Proving them wrong will be oh-so sweet, but how do you assume leadership of an entire department that's used to being crisis-managed?

Your brilliant track record in your previous company landed you this opportunity, but there, you were surrounded by friends and allies. You'd built solid relationships with your team and executive management. Questions begin swirling in your mind; Do you really have what it takes to lead them through this challenging period and onto bigger and better things? Will you be able to earn their trust and respect as a leader as quickly as possible? Can you shift the entire teams' focus onto areas of the business that are currently failing? Can you begin building a division all over again when you have no idea of what you're working with? It's more than just being able to identify the personality types and characteristics; it's a question of building trust, and doing it very quickly.

You can already feel the pressure of eyes watching every move you make from all sides. Your team isn't sure whether they can trust you or not, and those to whom you report have much higher expectations from the start. Your mandate requires you to ensure the sales division is operating like a well-oiled machine, or your head will be on the chopping block, and you know that you'll be facing the EXIT sign above the main entrance of the building.

You are already thinking of all the leadership skills you're not sure you currently possess, but you know they will be necessary if you'll be successful here. The first step is going to be earning the buy-in from those reporting to you, and gaining their trust as a leader. You know from experience that any insecurities or uncertainties displayed by you could be perceived as a weakness by the team. This may stand in the way of the entire department meeting goals set out by management. There's simply no way that you're going to allow this to happen during the six months you have. How do you meet these key objectives in any event? You know that there's no way to achieve this on your own.

Too many questions and uncertainties run through your mind, and you have so many decisions to face. Which do you tackle first, and how do you prove yourself to be a leader that a team wants to follow? Your management skills are sound because you've managed teams successfully in the past, but that was different. You'd been part of your previous firm for years, working your way up through the ranks and developing a reputation for yourself. You'd proven your worth to management and colleagues alike, and hit that glass ceiling where you could grow no further was devastating. You were looking for a bigger challenge, which is why you applied for this position; had you bitten off more than you can chew?

Admittedly, your management style and skills have not always been the greatest, and there has always been room for improvement. How could you learn to lead from the front when required, walk beside those that need guidance and direction, or gently nudge others from the back? Your stomach is in a knot, and you're beginning to feel overwhelmed. You don't know where to begin. You want to prove to the hiring manager and the management team that they made the right decision by bringing you on board, but it's going to mean learning as much about leadership as possible, and how to apply these skills to get the best out of your team.

Glancing over the motley crew, you're not even sure what personalities you've inherited or whether or not you'll be able to work with them. How can you determine where your current skills start and where they end? How can you learn to become a better leader, and to manage people better by empowering and inspiring them to be the very best they can be?

While this imaginary story may be applicable to someone who's already been a leader before, it may not apply to you. You may be wanting to get your feet wet and try your role at leadership, or you may be looking at studying towards becoming a leader someday. Wherever you find yourself, this book is for you. The following chapters are going to provide you with practical insights into leadership. What it is, and what it isn't. We will go through developing better relationships by connecting with people. After all, that's what leadership is all about. It will help you learn the art of effective communication with your team and those around you, so they'll follow you to the ends of the earth, no matter the cost. It will help you identify and enhance leadership skills you already possess and add those you still need.

This book is about learning to manage yourself first, managing others effectively, and learning to become a better leader. It's not just for all the leaders out there, it's also for supervisors, team leaders, managers, coaches, teachers, entrepreneurs, and employees—in short, this book is for anyone who would like to learn to strengthen their professional interpersonal relationships.

Some of the biggest challenges managers and leaders face in today's world is that they're qualified to supervise and lead on paper. They may have attended all the right training seminars and completed all the right courses, yet still don't possess the actual skills to lead. They don't know how to manage, motivate, and develop their employees. As individuals, they often stagnate in their roles, believing that 'once a leader, always a leader'. Rather than understanding that leadership is a skill that requires constant change, they become set in their ways.

This fast-paced world in which we live means that business is evolving and morphing at a frenetic pace. Leadership requires ongoing learning to ensure the best for those under you. Learning is not only necessary in times of crises, but rather should be a life-long commitment if you hold a leadership title. It's a way to embrace new technology and ideas, and should be seen as a means of strengthening teams and keeping abreast of innovative ways of doing things. It's keeping your finger on the pulse of all things "leadership" in your industry. Lack of learning results in stagnation, and no one flourishes or thrives under a stagnant leader.

Rapid changes across all industries result in many challenges for leaders, and while only a handful are listed below, you can understand why it's important to keep on top of whatever is happening within your industry. Most industries have their own unique set of challenges. Successful leaders can cut through all the bureaucratic red tape and get to the heart of the problem. The world of work has changed, and business is far from a time when men clocked in at the beginning of the day, reporting to their small cubicle, putting their heads down and working only to punch out at the end of the day, repeating the cycle all over again the following day. The humdrum boring monotony of this environment was what defined the world of work in the past, but it's most certainly not how things work today.

Now you have somewhat of an alphabet soup as various generations make up most of the workforce, and it's not only their outlook that's different. Gone are the days of the typical nine to five work routine with men in bowler hats and grey suits reporting for duty, never questioning anything because they were just happy to have work and receive a steady paycheck at the end of each month. Because of this, it makes perfect sense that the way people are led and managed should also undergo similar changes to meet the demands of the new world of work.

For the silent generation and baby boomers, most employees began and ended their careers within the same organization, retiring with their neatly packaged 401K and a gold pocket watch for 40 years of service. Millennials currently represent the largest workforce globally, and companies are being challenged in finding innovative ways to keep them. This turnover alone costs organizations and economies millions annually. This largest generation is constantly open to bigger and better things, so how do you learn to retain them and engage them?

Leadership skills are essential for everyone, and the great news is that it can be learned, meaning that there's no excuse for poor leadership. If leadership issues appear, they can be rectified and strengthened, rather than assuming that individuals are bad leaders. It's more cost-effective to identify areas of leadership that need to be strengthened and work on those, rather than disrupting entire departments or teams.

Thanks to emotional intelligence (EQ), we begin to understand ourselves and those around us better, which is crucial to leadership. You cannot expect others to follow you to where you have not been, or are unwilling to go on your own. Making use of emotional intelligence as part of your leadership strategy is another way to play to the strengths of individuals on your team.

There are many different styles of leadership to learn today, and just as many points of view. If you were to stop and ask 50 different individuals on the street, or run a snap survey within your organization, you're likely to find around 50 different answers to the same question. As a leader, you should remain as true to your natural leadership style as possible, if it's both effective and beneficial to your team and the company. If it isn't, then learning from a book like this can teach you how to make small adjustments to influence the lives of those you supervise in positive ways. This will impact the overall bottom-line of the business. Happy employees are productive employees. They are loyal employees and will give you everything they have. As their leader, recognition for great work should form part of your leadership strategy.

As a leader, personal goals are important. Set goals to learn new leadership skills to make your methods more effective. Strive to be liked and trusted by those reporting to you. Once you achieve this, you'll not only see better results from your team, but you can improve your retention strategies. Organizations with high staff turnover can end up spending millions of dollars retraining new hires and getting them up to speed. A happy staff is a productive staff, and teams collaborate better in this environment.

The main purpose of this book is to teach you how to master leadership skills that will motivate and inspire you and your team toward success. It's important to be able to define your department's organizational objectives—where are you going? How are you planning on getting there? And more importantly, why are you planning on moving in that direction? When individuals understand why they're doing something, they're more likely to buy-in and follow you. If they're left in the dark, then that's pretty much where they're likely to stay... in the dark, floundering!

Too many books about leadership are boring, repetitive, and the same as the rest. In this book, we will look towards providing you with concise, powerful, no-nonsense advice. The information is based on personal experience, research ranging from neuroscience, to science, to social psychology, and is backed up by scientific statistical data or analysis.

As you begin to improve and master your leadership skills, you will begin to see results from your colleagues. They will begin to trust you more and will follow you, doing whatever necessary to ensure objectives are met. Where you once may have doubted your abilities, you will feel more confident than ever before, and this will be seen within the relationships you have with those reporting to you.

This book is a must-read for all leaders, no matter the industry or leadership situation you find yourself in. Even as a parent, you will benefit from the information on these pages. There's not a moment to waste in deciding what you want from your life. Are you happy to stick with mediocrity and passing the time, or are you ready to kickstart your leadership style to the next level?

The choice now lies in your hands. Think about it. Where do you want to be a year from now? Do you want to be recognized as a leader that is on top of his or her game, changing things from the inside out? Or do you want to be left where you are now— still struggling to come to terms with what you could have, would have, or should have done? Are you ready to face defeat, refusing to grow as a leader, or are you prepared to dive into the following chapters, making each one of them your own? I look forward to having you join me, Peter Allen, author and business leader, on this life-altering leadership journey!

Chapter 1: Leadership Model

Unpacked

"The single biggest way to impact an organization is to focus on leadership development. There is almost no limit to the potential of an organization that recruits good people, raises them up as leaders and continuously develops them."

~ John C. Maxwell

The Model

The model that this book will follow is based on research from various scientific fields that have conducted extensive studies on leadership. Much has changed since the early 1900s, when behavioral science and psychology were all the rage. We are briefly going to consider some of the most influential psychologists who shaped leadership theories and are often referred to as the 'founding fathers' of behavioral science. Not all their theories were accurate or workable, and along with changes in the world of work, many of these psychologists altered their own opinions. Psychologists such as Freud, Thomas Carlyle, and many others had varying opinions on the subject, and as a result, streamlined the process of what it's become today. What few individuals consider, however, is that given the definition of leadership, many leaders existed throughout the period. Turning to history, one needs to consider individuals such as Caesar, Cleopatra, Genghis Khan, Alexander the Great, and Tutankhamen. At the time, these individuals were not always seen to be great leaders, although they led hundreds of thousands of individuals collectively. Much of their leadership characteristics were fear-based, rather than caring about the welfare of their people. (Maybe this is one of the reasons why they were born to lead during the eras they did.)

Working hand-in-hand with science is a way to identify certain leadership qualities, or strengths that an individual may have, yet these are not the final predictor as to whether or not you will be successful in a leadership role. There's much more to leadership than possessing great communication skills.

Despite some of the best possible predictive assessments, there is and always will be the human element involved in each leader, making it extremely difficult to put every single character in their own separate neat and tidy box. Statistical data analysis, whether strength and weakness-based, or gathered using longitudinal models, has been applied to the field of leadership for many decades. In keeping with this information, most of what we present will be based on these same models, in a concise way that offers you powerful, and applicable advice. Rather than skimming the surface, we will focus on those areas that will provide you with a better understanding of how your thoughts, decisions, and actions affect each of us as leaders in the 21st century. We will also consider areas where you may currently have limitations as a means of improving in these areas and turning each limitation into a strength. While this may sound like this is quite a simple process, it's not. Some limitations could take years to turn around. Being aware of them is an excellent place to start.

What is Leadership?

According to the Oxford online dictionary, 'leadership' is defined by the following words: authority, control, direction, guidance, influence, initiative, management, and supervision (Oxford, 2020).

Another definition that best describes it is by leadership expert, John C. Maxwell. He states in his bestselling book, *The 21 Irrefutable Laws of Leadership: Follow them and people will follow you*, that "The true measure of leadership is influence. Nothing more, nothing less" (Maxwell, 1998/2000). Being able to influence others and obtain followers could either be positive or negative, depending on who's doing the leading. Almost every industry has their own unique set of rules that govern the type of leadership they want. For the purpose of this book, we will look at leadership in business.

For most, it's the ability to lead others to achieve a set of goals or objectives that have been outlined by the company. It may be providing assistance and direction on how to get from one place to another, or being able to motivate a group of individuals towards common goals within an organization. While most are under the impression that you need a piece of paper, neatly framed, hanging behind your desk in a corner office before you are qualified to lead others, nothing could be further from the truth.

You can lead those around you purely through influence, rather than having to pressurize them to accept your way or the highway. There's more to leadership than meets the eye, and it's often easier to allow others to be in front.

It's more than learning to accept all the glory when things go right, and chastising others when things go wrong. A true leader gives credit where it's due, and then some. They get to know their team, discovering each's strengths and limitations and learning how to best work with them. Genuine leaders take an interest in the overall personal growth and development of their subordinates, or those for which they're responsible. They know how to accept blame when things go wrong and continue to keep their team motivated.

Being a leader means that you never have to make excuses for why things are not working out quite the way you would have liked them to. It's being able to analyze what went wrong along the way and gently guiding people back to where they need to be, helping them every step of the way. It's providing an open door, a listening ear, a shoulder to lean on, and the voice of reason when necessary. Leadership is being able to foresee things before they happen and doing whatever is required to prevent catastrophic fallout.

It does not mean giving in or caving at the first sign of opposition or defeat. Instead, it's about learning to stand your ground and standing up for those for which you're responsible, even though they may be in the wrong. It's giving them the benefit of the doubt first, and learning to help them through any periods where they may need to further learn and grow.

Leadership is about identifying and nurturing the talent within those individuals for which you're responsible. This means developing relationships with them where they are prepared to be open and honest with you at all times. They need to be willing to communicate with you openly and honestly. Rather than raising your own status above theirs as a leader, win them over to your side. If you attempt to rule over them, they will begin to create barriers between you and your team, and it's usually a long way back before you can guarantee cooperation and understanding. You want to be able to collaborate with everyone in your circle of influence.

Leadership is not about standing behind people, barking down orders with a bullhorn in one hand. It's not about the title that sits behind or beneath your name. Almost every organization like yours has similar management structures, so there are many others in the world carrying the same title as you. You don't even need a title to be an effective leader. Anyone can shout out orders to their workers and get fear-based results. That's not to say that you're getting the very best of what the employees are able to give you, or according to their individual capacity.

Stop reading for a few minutes and think about everyone in your department, your division, your branch, or your business? How much do you really know about each of them? Do you know what their greatest goals in life are? Do you even know what their ambitions within your organization are? Widen your outlook further, considering other divisions. Do you know your peers and co-workers? How about those that are on the same level as you? Do you know what their long- or short-term goals and aspirations are? Do you even know their names? While this may be a virtual impossibility for large organizations, small to medium enterprises should not have these problems. If you are meeting with your management team regularly, or even if you happen to sit on an Executive Committee at the Board level, it's still important to know what makes each of your colleagues get up and at it every day.

Being a leader is more than just picking up a larger paycheck than those you're responsible for—it's doing exactly that. Being responsible for them. Let's face it, it's easier to assume responsibility for others, genuine responsibility, only once you know them. Without this, it's merely posturing. It's putting on an act, playing a game, wearing a mask for the sake of either the 'higher-ups', or confusing yourself into thinking that you care.

Being a leader is not about pointing out faults and failures all day long. Instead, it's about working collectively towards uniting and strengthening individuals. The old saying, "you catch more flies with honey than with vinegar" springs to mind.

Being a leader doesn't mean that you get to bully others with scare tactics or threats; while it may be seen as a position of power, it should be one of humility instead. You should be acutely aware of your own shortcomings and failures and work on those. It's not always necessary to let your team in on these limitations, however, at times, that may be exactly what's required for them to be more tolerant, or cohesive. It may help them work together towards the achievement of common goals because they accept and understand that you, as an individual, are also human, with faults and failures, much the same as everyone else. It could help humanize you to them, instead of the rift between management and employees, that gap could be made much smaller.

So, how do you go about determining what type of leader you are, and how this is possibly going to assist you in your day-to-day working life? The first thing you need to do is take a long hard look in the mirror and identify those areas of your leadership style, and whether these are working with you, for you, or against you. Are there areas that need to be addressed and attended to? What are they? And what do you need to change to become the type of leader you would like to be?

Is your position within your organization and level of seniority a threat to you? Has it gone to your head? Has your senior management team assumed that you would magically find all the answers to be an effective leader just because you were promoted? (It's much the same argument as having the qualification and automatically assuming that this is going to make you an excellent leader).

Is leadership just for those in executive positions? Or can you become an effective leader right where you are (without a fancy promotion or pay increase)?

What You Need to Become A Leader

For psychologist and author, Kendra Cherry, and psychotherapist and author of *13 Things Mentally Strong People Don't Do*, Amy Morin, the following things should be accomplished in order to become a leader:

- The first and most important step when it comes to effective leadership is identifying and understanding your leadership style. Without this, it's impossible to know what your strengths and limitations are. In leadership, you need to be able to play to your strengths and look towards overcoming your limitations.

- Actively listen to those you supervise and communicate effectively with them.

- Be a positive role model and encourage those you lead to be innovative and creative. Help them discover how to think for themselves and "outside the box" rather than being another version of you.

- Be passionate about the work that you do, and through your positive attitude towards what needs to be done, encourage the participation of those you lead.

- Use rewards and recognition to motivate and encourage active participation from those within your team (Cherry & Morin, 2019).

How to Approach Leadership

According to Rita Balian Allen, a lecturer at Northeastern University, and Top Ten Executive Leadership Coaches in the USA, there are many different styles or approaches to leadership today. While there's no "one-size-fits-all" approach to leadership, it appears that the most prominent styles of leadership can be divided into five divisions. In a recent interview with Leslie Doyle, a writer from the University, she had these important points to say about leadership (Doyle, 2019). We will focus each of these in this section:

Participatory Leadership

This was previously referred to as a democratic leadership style, where employees are very much part of the decision-making process. As a participatory leader, a hands-on approach is adopted, and employees are recognized for the value they bring to the organization. These leaders encourage participation from their employees, allowing them to have a say in decisions and the way things are run. It's completely different from a regular "top-down" leadership strategy. An example of this type of leader is Martha Stewart and Donald Trump (Malsam, 2019).

Servant Leadership

This is the youngest of the different leadership styles and strategies. Servant leaders are more concerned with doing what's right for their workforce than what's right for them. They are focused on the needs of their people and building each employee as an individual by doing what's right for the team, individuals, and the community. They place themselves last, rather than first. This term was first coined by Robert K. Greenleaf in 1970. Well-known servant leaders include Steven Covey and Ken Blanchard (Wilbanks, 2018).

Studies have confirmed that this style of leadership yields higher returns and employees perform much better in this environment.

Situational Leadership

Developed by Ken Blanchard and Paul Hersey in 1969, they describe situational leaders as those who are able to assess the strengths of those within their team and to assign them tasks in line with their abilities. Communication between team members and leaders is essential for this type of leadership to be successful. Situational leaders manage their team according to strengths, limitations, and their motivations. Advancements within the team inspire individuals to perform better (Cherry & Morin, 2019).

Transformational Leadership

This type of leadership believes in increasing morale within a team and encouraging performance through connection. It's important for team members to be able to connect with the organization, as well as their own identities. Examples of transformational leaders include Winston Churchill and Steve Jobs.

Value-based Leadership

These leaders encourage members of their team to work towards the greater good of the shared values within an organization. This encourages teams to focus on the mission and vision of an organization, rather than following blindly. The leader themselves would uphold each of these core values, which would be built around the same values of the organization.

Can You Learn to Be a Good Leader?

There are so many ways to learn good leadership skills in this modern society, and yes, these skills can certainly be learned. Some of the basics could range from making a genuine impact on the lives of those you manage, to not showing favoritism among those you lead. According to Walden University, here are a few of their recommendations when learning to become a more effective leader:

- Don't be afraid to display the passion you have for what you do. Far too many leaders really love their work, yet they don't want their team, or those around them, to see it. You don't need to love absolutely everything about what you do to be passionate. Discover those facets of your work that you thoroughly enjoy doing, and focus your passion there. You can always build on it later.

- Good leaders realize that it's not about being popular all the time—they make hard decisions at the risk of being viewed as tough or unpopular. They know that there's no popularity contest when it comes to doing the right thing. And they choose to do the right thing every time, no matter how others feel about it.

- They're open to new ideas—the current market and world of work in which we live are forever changing, and it's only so long before another change comes along, as part of a natural way of doing things. They understand that their answers aren't always the right ones, and that's why they like to hear what others have to say so the best decisions are made, rather than the first decision, which may not be the best for all concerned.

- They adopt servant leadership skills and work for the good of their employees, rather than selfishly for themselves. Despite having to report to their manager(s), they strive to make the lives of their team better. This is done by creating an environment conducive to helping their employees to thrive. Happy employees are loyal and productive employees.

- They remain positive towards their staff, leading from the front. This means that they coach and support team members during difficult times, they praise their employees for positive contributions towards their work, and they stand by them when things are tough. Good leaders don't flip-flop between support, being supportive at certain times, and then changing whenever it suits them.

- Good leaders are respectful. They don't choose who they are going to respect. Some leaders are only respectful towards those to whom they report, while treating their employees poorly, as they decide to pull the "management" card. Good leaders respect both those above them, as well as those they lead.

- From the get-go, good leaders set the right example for their team to follow. They understand that leadership is not about them. Whenever something needs to be done, they will be the first to arrive in the morning, and usually be the last to leave at the end of the day. They don't expect their employees to do anything they're not prepared to do themselves.

- They accept that learning is a lifelong pursuit and do this not only by setting the right example for their team, but also encouraging team members to do the same. Most large organizations are prepared to invest in their employees to become better at what they do. If this is the situation within your organization, embrace these opportunities with both hands, and look for learning opportunities that will further your advancement within the organization. Learning is for everyone and should be treated that way (Walden University Blog, n.d.).

Chapter 2: Leadership Defined

"A true leader has the confidence to stand alone, the courage to make tough decisions, and the compassion to listen to the needs of others. He does not set out to be a leader but becomes one by the equality of his actions and the integrity of his intent."

~ Douglas MacArthur

Characteristics of Leaders

According to the Center for Creative Research, there are 10 characteristics that every successful leader possesses (Center for Creative Leadership Blog, 2019). They are:

The Art of Delegation

Being able to delegate is an important skill for any leader to master as early in their career as possible. This will help alleviate pressure when you have deadlines looming by sharing the workload between members of your team. Delegation is not passing your specific work onto other people. Instead, it's sharing a collective, team-based workload. When the entire team gets involved, relationships are strengthened. It allows your team to get to see who you are and understand you better, helping them realize that you are also human, just like them, and have days when pressure can build up. Opening up to your team through task delegation builds trust and mutual respect. You, as their leader, need to learn that you can trust them to complete whatever you assign them. You need to take opportunities that will help you to foster relationships, allowing them to work without being micromanaged. It lets them see that they are part of something bigger, a team that's valued, rather than a smaller cog in an organizational wheel.

Communicate Effectively

Communication is covered extensively in the final chapter. In terms of key ingredients to successful leadership in the 21st century, it's a vital ingredient.

Stand Up For Your Team

It takes tremendous courage to lead from the front. Even when you fear failure or ridicule, you need to stand up for yourself and your team. Fear often holds us back and can prevent us from achieving our goals as leaders, or collectively as a team. Many leaders ignore whatever negative or unhealthy things happening in their department in the hope that they will resolve themselves. This is the exact opposite of what courageous leaders need to be doing. Leaders should do more than bury their heads in the sand like an ostrich, and help resolve disputes, problems, and hiccups in the workplace before they are blown out of proportion. Fear makes these situations much worse than they need to be. As a leader, it is your job to step out of your comfort zone and be prepared to defend yourself, your team, your colleagues, or even your organization, no matter the cost.

Understanding Others

Having empathy towards those reporting to you, and learning to understand them is a key skill associated with emotional intelligence (EQ), and can be learned. Displaying these feelings in the workplace does not make you weak; it makes you human. It allows employees to see another side of you, one that cares what's happening in their lives and/or in the workplace. If you always expect your employees to give their best, this is a skill you need to practice and learn to master if you're not using it as a leadership technique already.

The Center of Creative Leadership completed a study by collecting and analyzing data from 6,731 managers in 38 countries. The purpose of the study was "to determine whether empathy can influence a manager's job performance." The results proved that those managers who displayed empathy towards their subordinates in the workplace were viewed by their own managers as being better performers. Emotional intelligence is all about our ability to connect. Using empathy and compassion allows you to understand and try to identify with the other individual's thoughts and feelings (Center of Creative Leadership Articles, n.d.-b).

Be aware of confusing empathy with sympathy. Sympathy is pitying someone without trying to place yourself in their shoes. Seeking understanding rather than proclaiming judgment is what you're aiming for as a leader. Learn to be truly present and pay close attention when employees are discussing problems with you.

Being Grateful

Too few leaders express sincere gratitude towards their employees for things such as work done, ideas shared, and putting in extra hours when not asked to do so to reach a deadline. Instead, leaders assume it's part of their work responsibility. While this may be true to a degree, in the sense that the employee is collecting a check at the end of every month, all the little extras are often what makes the difference. As a leader, saying thank you can lead to less stress and anxiety in the workplace, and greater self-esteem in your employees (Center for Creative Leadership Articles, n.d.-a).

There's a science behind expressing gratitude that goes hand-in-hand with both happiness and an overall sense of well-being. A controlled trial tested for connections between gratitude, sleep patterns, and subjective well-being. The trial was conducted using 119 young women over two weeks. Those randomly selected were asked to give thanks or express gratitude over the two-week period. The balance was requested to report on everyday events that occurred in their lives. At the end of this period, results indicated that sleep patterns improved, test subjects enjoyed an overall decrease in blood pressure. It further established that expressing gratitude was not only beneficial to the individual giving thanks, but also to the recipient (Jackowska et al., 2016).

A survey conducted by Glassdoor indicated that 80% of employees would work much harder in the workplace if their leader was more appreciative toward them and expressed gratitude. (Glassdoor Team, 2013).

Influence versus Control

Effective leadership is being able to influence others to do whatever is necessary while not trying to control them. As another EQ skill, it means that you should be able to connect with those reporting to you. Influence is the exact opposite of control or manipulation. It's not forcing your employees into subdued compliance, but convincing them to do things by choice on their own. It's allowing employees the freedom to follow, having built trust between you. George Hallenbeck, from the Center of Creative Leadership and the main contributor of their "Lead 4 Success" program says that "Without the ability to influence the heads, hearts, and hands of people, the truly important things in work and in life can't be achieved." (Center for Creative Leadership Articles, 2017). He goes on to identify the following four key skills:

Use Network Connections: You must have the ability to be able to network and connect with others, and then be able to make use of these networks in your favor.

Work Towards Common Goals: Understand how to get individuals moving towards common goals because they want to, not because they're being forced to.

Team Collaboration: Use authenticity and credibility to do what's best for the company. The organizational needs should always come first, above any personal agendas.

Influence with Trust: Use trust and influence to lead and direct individuals and teams. You can only achieve these things once your team trusts you and is ready to follow you wherever you lead them.

Honesty and Integrity

It feels as though this section should not have to be included, because as a leader, these two closely intertwined characteristics should come as a given. Unfortunately, not all leaders have unquestionable honesty and integrity. Leaders are responsible for the direction entire organizations move in, as well as what seems like an endless supply of other important business decisions. Integrity should be the first box to be checked off during an initial hiring interview. Not just for employees, but for every individual within an organization. The higher up the rung of the corporate ladder, the greater the level of honesty and integrity should be.

It's unsurprising, in the world in which we currently live, that dishonesty and scandal are found almost everywhere you look. Once again, studies have shown that for senior executives within organizations, "Integrity [is] the most important [strength] for top-level executives' performance" (Center for Creative Leadership Articles, n.d.-c).

Integrity is choosing to do the right thing even when nobody is watching you. It's being 100% trustworthy and ensuring your word is your bond. It's deciding what's right and what's wrong early in your life, and then never deviating into the murky depths of grey. As a leader, this should be unquestionable. As someone responsible for hiring those below you, if you use this as your standard, you should never have to question the integrity of anyone in your team.

Increased Learning Agility

Part of being a leader in the 21st century is recognizing that changes and advancements are going to require unlearning the old and relearning the new. Being able to tap into this skill is what's referred to as "learning agility." According to Megha Singh from the Learning and Development Division of Mecer,

> *"Learning agility is the ability to continually and rapidly learn, unlearn, and relearn mental models and practices from a variety of experiences, people, and sources, and to apply that learning in new and changing contexts to achieve desired results. It is a mind-set and corresponding collection of practices that allow people to continually develop, grow, and utilize new strategies that will equip them for the increasingly complex problems they face in their organizations."*

In his 1970s book, *Future Shock*, Alvin Toffler made the following quotation that was way ahead of its time when he said, "The illiterate of the 21st century will not be those who cannot read and write, but those who cannot learn, unlearn and relearn" (Toffler, 1970).

Those who are especially good at embracing learning agility are usually more actively involved in what's happening within their organization. They are able to come up with new ideas fairly quickly, and don't have problems implementing solutions that work. In addition to the above, they come off as being more resilient and calm in the workplace. As leaders within this type of environment, they not only encourage their staff to become involved in learning agility behavior, but they also provide various solutions where their employees can benefit from this extra learning.

- The benefits of learning agility include improved productivity within the various departments and the organization as a whole.

- There's an increase in the number of employees who are ready to face whatever challenges are thrown their way as part of changes within the workplace.

- Why is learning agility necessary for today's workplace?

There are technological advancements taking place that are shaping the future of the world of work at the moment. This means advancements in artificial intelligence (AI) and robotics; technological advancements require constant innovation and having to reinvent not only business models, but often entire positions within business. This is thanks to a marketplace that is currently expanding due to globalization (this brings its own specific highly competitive dynamic with it).

Millennials, who make up the largest population of the current workforce, are constantly rebelling against the old way of doing things. They not only want to work differently, but demand that the entire work landscape changes to suit their specific needs. Naturally, within the workplace, the division bearing the brunt of all these changes is Human Resources (HR). They not only need to look for those who display the potential to be able to learn, unlearn, and relearn, but also those who can get along with others (Singh, 2020).

Four steps that can be taken to approach learning agility are:

Looking: Finding the right place to gain the knowledge or skills required to complete future tasks.

Understanding Learning: It's not just important to find where to acquire these new skills or knowledge, but you need to understand what you are learning. This can be done by questioning things you don't understand until you reach a point where you do.

Internalizing Learning: Make whatever you've learned your own. This key component to learning agility will help you to move onto the following step!

Application of New Learning: The point of learning new skills can only be valuable if you can apply what you've been taught. It should allow you to improve your current working environment, whether this means improving on processes, or working better with your team. Whatever new skill you are fortunate enough to learn or relearn needs to be applied. If it so happens that you were the only individual within your team fortunate enough to attend a training environment, share the knowledge gained with your team.

The entire emphasis of learning agility is to make things better for everyone. By sharing with your team, there will always be someone within your inner circle in the workplace who can back you up, or help out if you aren't there for some reason. Learning agility should be a skill adopted by everyone, and not just shared with a select few.

Admiration and Respect

In this context, we are discussing the leaders' respect for those they lead. While respect is often referred to as a two-way street, as their leader, you cannot expect your employees to deliver their best work if they feel that you don't respect them as individuals or collectively as a team. There are many ways you can show your employees that you respect them, or that they're valued members of the team as a collective group of individuals.

For teams to work more effectively as a cohesive unit, they need to feel your support as their leader. They also need to feel that they are respected and supported as part of a team. Here are some ways that you, as their leader, can physically show this support:

- Having an open-door policy when teams are working on projects. Indicate that you are available to assist in any way you possibly can. It's important that you actually mean this, and aren't just paying them lip-service.
- Providing an environment where you're prepared to listen to what your team has to say. This is more than pretending to listen and be concerned. It's allowing your employees to use you as a sounding board to bounce ideas off of. It's recognizing them for their input as part of the team, and the entire team's participation when it comes to projects. A practical tip, when it comes to active listening, is to allow the other person to finish speaking first, before interrupting with an answer.

Learning to trust your team is another way to show your respect for them. According to Social-Emotional Intelligence and Soft-Skills Training expert, Stefan Jacobson, the most important time to be honest and open with your team is when you need to provide feedback that's not always comfortable. Times like these are never easy, however, they are necessary for teams and individuals alike to be able to grow (Jacobson, 2019).

Jacobson also states that one of the most effective ways to show respect towards your employees is by encouraging them to participate in important projects and providing them with honest feedback. Not everyone is prepared to leave their comfort zones to step out of the shadows that they're used to. Often, team members are happy to keep their heads down without anyone even noticing them. They fly under the radar constantly, remaining silent in company meetings, even preferring to hide behind their colleagues. What's often sad about these individuals is they are highly intelligent and could have a lot to contribute. Encourage them to participate in group discussions. Make them feel comfortable and confident. As you do so, they will feel more inclined to contribute again in the future.

Self-awareness

Self-awareness is another EQ-based leadership skill, although it's one that's inward-facing. This means that rather than considering what's happening around you, you need to be in touch with your thoughts and feelings instead. According to Michelle Kankousky from the Learning and Development Consultant for Insperity, there are several strategies that you can incorporate into your leadership strategy that deal with self-awareness. Some of these are (Kankousky, 2017):

Understanding Your Strengths and Weaknesses: This is never a comfortable subject to have to face, yet we all have both strengths and weaknesses. The idea when working with self-awareness is to learn how to play to your strengths and overcome your weaknesses at the same time. This is easier said than done, of course (if you've ever tried to overcome a weakness or limitation, you know what I mean). It's only through understanding these and identifying possible triggers that you can begin to overcome them one at a time.

Ask for Feedback: As important as it is for you, as a leader, to provide your team with both positive and negative feedback for them to grow, invite them to provide you with feedback on your leadership. Remember that once you do this, you should be prepared for the occasional negative feedback, and accept it without bitterness and bias. Afterall, you want to improve as a leader—and this is how you do it. Feedback could also come from your peers and those above you. It's also recommended that this happens more often than an annual review. If there are specific areas you need to change, it's better knowing about them as soon as possible.

Be Open-Minded: This is an excellent way to get to know your team better and to really learn to collaborate more effectively. If you are one of these leaders that likes everything to be just perfect before moving ahead with a project, you are going to (and probably have) face a lot of disappointments in your life. Keep an open mind with your team. Allow them to contribute and share their ideas during brainstorming or problem-solving sessions. Consider how each individual team member operates and plays to their strengths. Although you are the leader, the group as a whole should come first.

Chapter 3: Leading Yourself

"Control is not leadership; management is not leadership; leadership is leadership. If you seek to lead, invest at least 50% of your time in leading yourself—your own purpose, ethics, principles, motivation, conduct. Invest at least 20% leading those with authority over you and 15% leading your peers."

~ Dee Hock

Set the Example

Good leaders set the example for those reporting to them to follow. As they do, they allow those they lead to learn from them and inspire them to be better in their own jobs. Leaders understand that team(s) are watching them, manager(s) are watching them, and it would be unreasonable to expect others to follow you if you're not prepared to lead by example. Setting this example means putting in extra hours whenever necessary without moaning or complaining. It's setting the right example in every area of the job.

Make sure your team can see you and knows what you are doing. If you're putting in extra hours, be sure they're aware that you're prepared to do this and are doing it for the benefit of the team. This shouldn't be done in a way that makes them feel inferior. Instead, invite them to join in these activities, making it easier for them to follow you as a leader.

Leaders aren't afraid of helping team members feeling overwhelmed with their workloads. This forms part of servant leadership. If others realize you see what's happening in your department and aren't afraid of assisting if there's a major project that needs working on, the more they will be inclined to help one another.

Why do you want to set an example of leadership for those in your team to follow? Do you want greater influence over them, popularity, or do you have selfish motives? In leadership, there will always be someone watching everything you do. While it may not always be the same individual doing the watching, someone is noticing the hours you put in, the number of coffee breaks you take, the way you dress, how you address your superiors and your subordinates—everything is being watched and analyzed. You may even be the owner of the organization and feel that because of this designation, you should be precluded from this kind of scrutiny. Unfortunately, in this instance, you are probably scrutinized even more carefully, and not just by individuals within your own organization.

Setting the right example needs to be visible. Without it, what's the point of doing the work if nobody can see what you're doing? As a leader, your team of employees should recognize your contributions towards the team. Something to remember as a leader is that actions can have a far greater impact than words ever could.

Learn from Experience

Criticism and Advice

Accepting advice or criticism can be tough since most of the time, we believe we're right. Becoming a leader isn't achieved automatically or overnight. You cannot step into a leadership role and get everything 100% right the first time. Remember what it felt like receiving sage advice from those who were more experienced in management than you? Hold onto those feelings. If you were fortunate enough to have a mentor or a career coach that helped you through your early leadership years, remember how much of that learning was by trial and error. If you're a brand new leader, please understand that coping with advice and criticism is a skill that you will need to develop, but it's one you will use throughout your life, because you will never please everyone all the time. Focus on how you can improve and ask for feedback from those who are older and wiser than you (this is not necessarily an age dynamic, look for those who have more leadership experience). Receiving this advice will keep you on your toes and continue to move forward, rather than stagnating as a leader and accepting the status quo as good enough.

Additional Workload

Do you recall when you first had additional responsibilities added to your leadership role and how this made you feel? That sense of being overwhelmed, unsure of which task needed to be managed first? Tap into these memories and how you handled the situation. This is not to say that the way you dealt with it was always the best. What is undeniable, however, is that you gained valuable knowledge and experience from it and this allowed you to learn.

Part of being a successful leader means being flexible, willing, and able to deal with whatever is thrown your way without flinching or losing sight of the end goal. How you react to your supervisors' requests to take on extra work is exactly how your team will react when you assign additional work to them. Learning coping skills is part of a learning curve, without collapsing into a heap feeling overstressed, overworked, or wanting to throw a pity-party because you're feeling underappreciated. Instead, use this to your advantage by delegating additional work to your team, while closely monitoring them so they don't feel the same way you did the first time it happened to you.

Feedback

Apart from asking members of your team for regular feedback, ask clients by interacting with them. This could provide, not only you, but your entire organization with some valuable insights as to how you are doing as a leader, how your team is doing, and how the organization as a whole is performing. You cannot fix something unless you know that it's broken. You cannot improve who you are or anyone else in your department unless you know how you are doing. Focus on each area of your business that interacts with customers and channel your energies into identifying what's working for them, and what's not. Use the information you receive to improve what you are doing so both you and your team can learn together, grow together and be better, together.

Crisis Management

How you've managed crises in the past can teach your team members how to deal with it effectively as a team. Share your previous experiences with them, letting them know that you've been in a similar situation before, and tell them how you handled it. Guaranteed, you would not have gotten it right the first time around. You can probably share several experiences with your team when you've made monumental mistakes. What's most important here would be what you learned from your mistakes. These should serve as lessons for your team on "what not to do." Crisis management brings intense emotions with it. Share your feelings with the team without allowing any of these emotions to cloud effective leadership.

Diversity Management

Remember when you were first introduced to working with individuals from different backgrounds. While this should never influence the way we lead a group of people, it often does. Accept that everyone is unique, and their individuality should be celebrated rather than having differences highlighted. Differences often make for valuable and unique teams. Differences aren't always physical attributes. They could also be whether or not we encourage inclusion in our teams. As a leader, if you recognize that certain team members are more introverted than others, it's your job to make them feel that what they have to say matters.

Mistakes

Remember mistakes that you've made, or where you've made a poor judgment call and the consequences to those decisions. Use this experience as a reminder to be more considerate in decision-making. Part of the human condition is that we all make mistakes. What's most important, though, is to remember the cost of poor decision-making. This could be a financial cost, a time cost, or even a reputational cost. Poor decision-making will always occur, but it should occur less frequently the longer you're in a leadership position if you're using previous experience as a predictor of future behavior.

No form of failure feels good. Admitting that we've failed is worse. If it's any consolation, every successful leader has a string of failures behind them because it's one of the best ways to be able to learn, grow, and progress. The most important part of failure is learning from it. If we keep making the same mistakes repeatedly, we've learned nothing, and we should go back to the beginning. The best way to learn from failure is to dissect the event, our actions, as well as the outcome or result. Once this has been done, it becomes easier to identify what went wrong so we don't repeat the same mistake again. Sharing what we learned with others is another way of preventing similar mistakes.

Finding Solutions

Tapping into past experiences to make you a better leader is not always negative. Coming up with successful solutions to problems you've encountered in the past can encourage you to be consistent and tenacious in finding solutions for current problems. If you've succeeded in the past, you can do so again in the future.

Dealing With Change

Dealing with change can be disruptive, especially if it's management changes where you've been close to someone for a number of years. Think about previous times when you've had to work through change in the past, and how you managed to do so successfully. It may be worth remembering your first day walking into the organization when you were the bright, shiny, new penny. Leaders complete with their different styles will come and go, and being able to recall how you've dealt with it before willassist your teamwork through it effectively now.

Initiative

Taking initiative can be challenging, especially in an event where it's not encouraged, but it's necessary. Think about times when you were forced to come up with creative solutions towards solving problems. This may make you dig deep and challenge parts of yourself that you are maybe not comfortable with, especially if you have worked in an environment where you were told what you needed to do and when you needed to do it.

Learning New Things

Leadership means being prepared to learn new things and broaden your scope of experience. As we've listed each of the above items, there are probably many more that have sprung to mind. There will be times when you'll be forced to think about situations in the past and make use of them by bringing all this experience together. Experience is something that nobody can ever take away from you. It can either be used to your advantage to make you a better leader, or it can be left to stagnate, which results in having almost no value whatsoever. Experience is something that you're able to pass onto your team.

Expertise

We may not always realize how much valuable knowledge and expertise we have gained over the years that can be applied to everyday work situations. Not all experience needs to come from the workplace. You may have learned something regarding brainstorming or active listening when you were a student. These skills never leave you, and you tap into them on a regular basis. Just because they happen to be used as part of your leadership skills, doesn't mean that you must acquire them in the workplace. Many of these are soft skills, which are "personal attributes that enable someone to interact effectively and harmoniously with other people" (Oxford English Online, 2020).

Some of the most important lessons that you can learn as a leader often come from mistakes that colleagues make. Pay attention to what they do, especially things that either work or don't work. In doing so, you're able to avoid following in their footsteps.

Leading Is Doing

There are several important points to be made when it comes to actually "doing" and leading effectively. Deciding to do the work yourself and taking assignments back from your team will prevent them from learning, growing, making their own decisions, and making their own mistakes. It's important for them to be able to gain this experience for themselves by doing, rather than having a leader who is controlling.

Some leaders become frustrated because they're not necessarily seeing the results that they would like from their team. Instead of using this as a teaching or training experience, they adopt the attitude that it's easier to do the work themselves. Leading from the front means leading by example, while not doing the work. It's being able to encourage and inspire employees to deliver their very best work.

Leading from the front means being prepared to set the best example for your team to follow by respecting your superiors and the chain of command within your organization. It requires an effective delegation and follow-through process once this has been done. It's building your team by fostering relationships of trust. Once you've delegated the work, step back and allow those you lead work with what you've assigned to them.

Employees will mimic leaders when it comes to working habits. It can also be seen in your attitude towards those you lead. Are you genuinely concerned about their well-being and happiness in the workplace? Are they aware that you care enough about them that you'd prefer to see them grow into leaders themselves? This means stepping back and allowing them to fail occasionally. Allowing them to do so gives you the opportunity to mold them into potential leaders themselves, and so the cycle of leadership development begins to take effect.

If you commit to rewarding your team or even individual employees for work completed, such as projects, meeting production targets, or achieving a sales goal, be sure to follow through as promised. This will allow those you lead to recognize you as someone of your word and will earn greater respect from each of them. Remember what you were like before stepping into a leadership role; you may gain some valuable insight as to what your team is currently going through right now.

Chapter 4: Leadership Toughness

"Don't wait until everything is just right. It will never be perfect. There will always be challenges, obstacles and less than perfect conditions. So what? Get started now. With each step you take, you will grow stronger and stronger, more and more skilled, more and more self-confident, and more and more successful."

~ Mark Victor Hansen

Mental Toughness

The pressure is building up, deadlines are hanging over your head, or it's inching closer towards month-end and you still have targets to be met. Management is beginning to apply greater force than you're used to. Your next steps are determined by your degree of mental toughness. Whether you choose to sink or swim depends on whether or not you can persevere, remaining productive during this period. The alternative is to give up and allow the current to drag you down with it. Can mental toughness be taught, and if so, how do you learn it and apply it to your current work environment?

Ask athletes across various sports and almost all of them will tell you that most of their success has come through mental toughness coaching. Once they have successfully developed how to apply mental toughness in any situation, they can consistently do their best despite the circumstances they find themselves in.

For leaders to be successful when faced with challenges, they need to be flexible and display a degree of mental plasticity. This means being prepared to change direction at a moment's notice without digging your heels in. Instead, it's welcoming fresh, new ideas that may present solutions to getting the job done, rather than insisting that the old way is the right way. It's opening your mind to new ideas that may just be better than the old ways.

The acquisition of new skills and knowledge comes with mental toughness because you're prepared to admit that you don't know everything. For business leaders, this is often one of the most difficult admissions to make. So, where should you be turning for this new advice or knowledge? This depends on the situation, but the fact is that the leader is prepared to look for new answers to new problems. Because we're faced with brand new challenges daily, we need to continue searching for innovative solutions. Gaining the required knowledge may mean re-learning skills that we've forgotten.

Part of successful business leadership is continuous growth and learning results in growth, helping teams and organizations move forward towards their ultimate goals. Learning should be a life-long event, and as a leader, you can hand this ambition to those reporting to you.

Resilience is at the very heart of mental toughness, as this provides the flexibility to bounce back, especially in the event of failure (which happens to all of us). It's being able to get up every single time you get knocked down or defeated, no matter what. Resilience is a choice that you make and how you plan to face change whenever it's presented to you. It's your mental, emotional, and physical response to defeat, or other obstacles that happen to be placed in front of you. Resilience is looking for opportunities where you can learn and grow from a situation, rather than blaming others.

Response time can be a major contributing factor to mental toughness. Those who sit around and wait, or mull back and forth over ideas before deciding can impact the overall outcome. With mental toughness, it's important that you come up with a solution as quickly as possible. Even if it's not the right decision, it gives you a platform to continue searching for solutions from. Wasting time is a valuable commodity that most businesses don't have the luxury of doing, especially in the competitive world in which we're currently living. Those who can make rapid decisions to resolve problems can remain one step ahead of their opposition.

Mentally tough leaders have a strength that runs deeper than their ability to remain mentally and physically alert and responsive during challenging times. These strengths give them the tenacity to see each challenge through to the end no matter what. It's the ability to remain focused on whether you win or lose. Mental toughness should be a skill that every successful leader acquires. According to Leadership Strategist, Tony Ewing, there are certain things that leaders with emotional toughness never do (Ewing, 2020):

- They never make important decisions when they're feeling emotional. Scientifically, it's been proven that cognitive control affects the decision-making process, and this is influenced by our emotions. As a result, any major decisions should rather be made when you're feeling both rational and clear-headed. (Inzlicht et al., 2015).

- Those who are mentally tough don't delay making decisions. They don't need to waste time trying to come up with the right solution to the problem. They consider all the facts available and decide on what their intuition tells them will be best for all parties concerned.

- They don't jump to conclusions without background information. Those who are mentally tough ensure they have as many facts, figures, and information available to them as possible. They identify when insufficient information is available to make a decision, and will remove themselves from the decision-making process. They don't need the information to support their conclusion. They consider the pros and cons of the given situation and decide based on the information available.

- They don't need the approval of others as part of their decision-making process. They're not swayed by having to be popular or not.

- They accept reality and don't assume they can never be wrong. They operate from a viewpoint of reality where everyone is a part. They don't separate themselves from everyone else with a different viewpoint.

- They don't avoid change; instead, they embrace it as change means growth (Ewing, 2020).

When Leaders Are at Their Best

As part of this section, we are going to be looking at several ways where you can benchmark your own performance as a leader by asking yourself several key questions and being brutally honest with the answers. It's only once you do this that you can be certain whether you're at your best as a leader.

Are Your Team Members Thriving or Stagnating?

One of the most important questions to ask yourself as a benchmark for successful leadership is to assess whether the individuals reporting to you are thriving or stagnating. You need to monitor them often by spending time with them individually, following up on work they've been assigned to do, and conducting regular feedback interviews or meetings with them. Employing EQ skills will help you assess the body language of the team. This will allow you to gain a better perspective on how they feel towards you as their leader, and towards their work. Mastering emotional intelligence skills will benefit you throughout your career, and not just while leading your current team.

By getting to know each member of your team individually, they will open up and share their hopes and dreams with you, as well as their goals for the future. To lead them successfully, you need this information (even though it may seem unimportant at the time). By truly connecting with them on such a personal level, you will not only have things to discuss that are outside the realm of "work," but you will display a genuine concern for those you lead, rather than a superficial relationship where you get the corner office and have minimal communication with your team. The ability to connect personally will allow you to encourage the achievement of their goals, whether personal or professional.

Do your team members know what your top priorities for the year are? If not, why not? As the leader of a team that has shared visions and goals to be working towards, it should be automatically "given" that your goals and priorities are closely aligned with those of the organization, and that your team knows exactly what these are. Similarly, getting to know those for which you're responsible will help you to gain a better understanding of their hopes and dreams and career aspirations. Don't be afraid of letting your team members get close enough to you to know exactly where you want to be in both the short- and long-term. Too many leaders assume the leadership role should separate them from their team. Successful leaders work collaboratively and collectively with those under them. They have their sights set on a common goal, and aren't afraid to share this knowledge with others that can assist them in their quest.

Do your team members feel that they can come to you with anything, or are they afraid of you as a leader, especially when it comes to failing? Let's face it; none of us likes to fail. It makes us feel horrible, and we begin to question our abilities, and get all hung-up in self-loathing, pity, blame, and all those other self-defeating thoughts and emotions. If you are the best you can be as a leader, this team member won't be afraid of failure because they would know that it presents an opportunity for them to learn and grow, and that even you, as their leader, have failed from time to time.

Working with a team that is functioning out of fear, rather than loyalty and passion, won't produce the best results. You will constantly have them second-guessing themselves and one another, as well as your ability to lead from the front in an ever-changing world of work. Ideally, they are looking for a leader that is both accountable and responsible for those they lead. These two words hold such importance for organizations and teams alike because so many leaders aren't prepared to accept accountability or responsibility for those they manage.

It's become far easier to point fingers in the direction of others, rather than accepting accountability, looking for solutions that can be applied to the problem and acting responsibly. These are the characteristics of a true leader. Someone who's not afraid of failing, and instead recognizes failure as part of leadership and a way to further develop his or her leadership skills.

Successful leaders are open to new ideas and welcome these from members of their team. They realize that they don't know everything that there is to know on every subject. This would be an impossible feat, however, by looking towards those of their team who possess increased knowledge in certain areas, so they're sure to receive the right input. This is especially effective when working closely to brainstorm, come up with fresh new ideas, or overcome a specific problem or challenge that you may be facing at the time.

Excellent leaders are more focused on passing on the positive skills they have learned as a leader as a means of creating more leaders or successors. The thought of coaching or mentoring others into leadership roles doesn't threaten them because they understand that part of the growth process will mean learning to let go and move on at some stage. What better legacy to be able to leave behind than someone who has developed strong leadership attributes at the side of an effective leader?

Successful leaders are empathetic and kind. They aren't judgmental, and accept that people are human and are subject to many things in life. They aren't afraid of showing this "softer" side of their personality because they don't believe that it makes them weak. Instead, they recognize that it makes them more human for those they lead.

True leaders are flexible in their leadership style. They are prepared to shift into different management modes, depending on what each situation calls for. These leaders can also adjust their management style to suit the individuals under them. In some instances, team members can work on their own, totally unsupervised, and unmanaged, while others need to be micromanaged and their work needs to be checked several times to ensure that it's correct before anything can be done with it. It's being able to successfully morph between the two, without losing credibility with your team. Ideally, these shifts would be so subtle that your team hardly even notices the difference.

Successful managers constantly provide direct feedback on individual performance. This is done regularly and privately so that individuals who need firmer encouragement aren't embarrassed in front of their colleagues. This is a characteristic that will always hold you in good stead and you should reward your team members openly with any awards or recognition, and chastise those who need correction or redirection in private. Nobody benefits from public humiliation; all that happens is the leader loses credibility in the eyes of the team.

Great leaders manage to keep a positive attitude, no matter what's going on around them—this, in turn, keeps the team productive and motivated. These leaders can successfully hide when things are going sideways or if they're facing a personal crisis. All that's important is ensuring that bottom-line results are achieved, and achieved consistently. Leaders encourage those reporting to them to constantly be bottom-line conscious in all that they do. It's easy for employees to get caught up in the work environment that they don't see the business operating costs as part of the organization. Great leaders can point these out to their employees in such a way that they are prepared to collaborate towards trimming these unseen expenses.

Excellent leaders are prepared to step out of their comfort zone and do uncomfortable things. Some of these may be making tough decisions that affect the business organization (such as hiring or firing). Whatever it is, when times are uncomfortable and the pressure is on, mental toughness, as discussed previously, as well as being strong enough emotionally to make difficult decisions, becomes apparent.

Great leaders are results-centric. This means that they're all about producing results, no matter what it takes. Whether these are production results, sales results, customer service indices, whatever they may be, true leaders understand that without a marketplace, there would be no business organization, and they protect it at all costs. They also make it their business to understand all areas of the business operation, so they remain informed and up-to-date with any and all aspects of the organization.

Excellent leaders have clear employee goals and expectations. Because they know each of their employees, they know what to expect from them, how far they can push them, and whether their employees are coping successfully or not.

Great leaders are prepared to teach their employees how things should be done instead of giving orders and expecting employees to understand. They don't expect employees to do anything that they cannot do themselves (unless the employee is a specialist and has been hired for this purpose).

As leaders, their vision is clearly defined, and they understand their own motivation. They willingly share this information with those on their team to inspire and motivate others to follow.

Leaders are humble yet curious creatures. They give credit where credit is due, but are willing to take the fall for their team whenever necessary. They seldom think of themselves first, instead; it's about the organization and the team, rather than the leader.

Chapter 5: Extraordinary Leadership

"Always dream and shoot higher than you know you can do. Don't bother just to be better than your contemporaries or predecessors. Try to do better than yourself."

~ William Faulkner

Making Extraordinary Things Happen

Discovering how to hone your talents and skills as an extraordinary leader means being able to roll up your sleeves and getting into the trenches with your staff. Having interviewed numerous successful, forward-thinking CEOs, performance strategist and author of *The Genius Habit*, Laura Garnett has identified the following as key elements in your leadership strategy of moving from good to great (Garnett, 2015):

Allow Others to Lead

It's difficult allowing those you lead to take the reins for a while for them to learn and grow, not only as individuals, but maybe as part of their career aspirations. As their leader, you should know to whom you can entrust this within your group. Maybe you'd like to rotate the leadership responsibility with each team member, allowing them to discover for themselves what leadership skills they possess. You may find some individuals who will automatically shrink backward at this opportunity. Don't force them or make them feel even more uncomfortable by calling them out. Not everyone is born to lead. There are many who are quite comfortable following and doing what is required of them. As their leader, you should know who these individuals are already. Assign them some other tasks that are better suited to who they are.

Ask Critical Questions

Asking the right questions at the right time will provide valuable insights into the team and how it progresses as a cohesive unit. Asking the right questions allows you to put those you lead first. It can remove you from being too close to a situation (allowing you to see things from a different perspective) to come up with creative solutions. Asking questions will help you understand your team better as well as gaining a clearer knowledge of their hopes and aspirations for the future.

Focus on Diversity and Overcoming Bias

Extraordinary leaders respect the thoughts and opinions of those they lead. They don't assume that their way of thinking is always correct. Because of this, they are open to new thoughts, suggestions, and innovative ideas from those they manage. They embrace the diversity of thought, recognizing that we are each unique and don't need to think the same way to be extraordinary. According to Timothy Wilson, a psychology professor at the University of Virginia and author of *Strangers to Ourselves: Discovering the Adaptive Unconscious*, the brain, is bombarded by an average of 11 million pieces of information at any given moment. Wilson confirms that because we are only able to process around 40 pieces of this information, the brain creates shortcuts and works from historical data and past experiences to make present assumptions. As leaders, we often settle for the first answer to a problem, purely because it falls into one of these 40 suppositions. This doesn't mean that better answers aren't out there, and we should be challenging ourselves to find them (Porter, 2014).

Lead by Example

One of the most important elements of leadership is doing what you expect others to do and leading through your own example. Members of your team will be quick to follow whatever you do. They look to you as a source of inspiration and guidance. If your example is one of egocentric behavior, that's exactly what you're going to get out of your team. On the other hand, if you are passionate about your work, you have a strong moral code and work ethic, you're reliable and dependable, then this is exactly what your team will present to you.

Much of what your team members do will be a mirror-image to your behavior. If there's something there that you don't like, or happens to be disrupting the functionality of the team, it may be time to look inwards and examine your own work ethics.

Play to The Strengths of Your Team

As a leader over a team, it's your job to understand each team member thoroughly. This means knowing what their hopes, dreams, and aspirations for the future are. Where do they see themselves in a year from now? Five years from now, and so on. Are they looking to someday take over for you, being able to manage their own team, or do they have greater aspirations that have nothing to do with their current position? By knowing and understanding your team, you should know exactly what their strengths and limitations are. What do they want to accomplish over the short-term? How can you, as their leader assist them to reach this goal?

As you work with your team, allow each of them to play towards their strengths. If someone is great at negotiations, place them in a position where this skill can be used to its maximum capacity. Others don't necessarily like the limelight. Perhaps they prefer working in the background crunching numbers. That's okay, there's a place for these individuals. Don't force them into the foreground to see whether they can handle pressure—you already know the answer. They may well be able to handle extreme pressure when it comes to numbers and deadlines. Give them the opportunity to shine, doing what they're best at doing. If you stick to this recipe, your business will succeed all the time.

Reignite Your Own Leadership Flame

We are all entitled to have bad days when things don't seem to go right, and we question our own ability to lead others. Remember that you are also only human, and because of this, you need to arm yourself with those skills and attributes that will help you to pull yourself out to these ruts whenever they appear. Learn to recognize the signs for whenever you feel yourself being pulled off your game. Set a game plan for whenever this happens to help reignite your leadership flame. Only you will know what works for you. For some, it takes quiet introspection, analyzing and diagnosing whatever has gone wrong and trying to come up with creative ways to fix these mistakes. For others, it's being able to use a mentor or trusted friend as a sounding board to bounce ideas around. Others like to discuss this with their team, allowing them to peek behind the curtain briefly to see that you are still only human after all.

One important takeaway from this section is that we all face downtimes as leaders. This will always be the case. What's important is to try and recognize what sets these lows off and how to deal with each of them effectively. Knowing this will assist you to snap out of it much quicker the next time it occurs. Being aware of yourself, your emotions, and your way of thinking to display high emotional intelligence, a characteristic that you want to develop and be able to share with those you lead (Garnett, 2015).

The Practices of Excellent Leadership

In this section, we are going to focus our attention on some of the world's greatest leaders, considering what has made them great, what sets them apart, and what they are possibly doing differently than other leaders in a rapidly changing world.

Jeff Bezos, Founder, and CEO of Amazon

Further to a statement made by Jeff Bezos to the U.S. House of Representatives at the end of July 2020, Bezos tells his own story about how he created Amazon out of his garage some 26 years ago. His childhood was not the easiest, his mother became pregnant as a teenager, and it was only thanks to the tenacity of his grandfather that she could continue with her classes. Moving onto college, she went to night school, taking classes that would allow her to take her small child along with her.

Jeff was adopted by Miguel, a Cuban immigrant who was sent to America in search of the "American Dream," by his parents shortly after Castro took over. Having obtained a scholarship to study, he met Jeff's mom, Jackie, as they attended the same college. Miguel and Jackie married, and Jeff was adopted at the age of four. Between this time and when Jeff was 16, he was fortunate enough to spend most of his summers on his grandparents' ranch in Texas. There, he was taught the value of hard work. He learned that you couldn't just rely on someone coming out to repair things as they broke. With the ranch situated in the middle of nowhere, Jeff watched his grandfather come up with innovative solutions to solve problems that often looked as though they were impossible.

The lessons Jeff learned from his grandfather spurred him onto attempting his own inventions as a teenager.

By 1994, Jeff had visualized Amazon. Creating an online bookstore with millions of books appealed to him. It was impossible at the time. Although he was already working full-time at an investment company in New York, he could not help but answer the call of destiny pulling him towards his dream. His manager tried to convince him to stay once he had decided to resign, by encouraging him to think about it, rather than jumping in blindly. The answer Jeff gave him two days later was that he would rather attempt his dream and fail, than live a life not knowing what would have happened had he been given the opportunity.

Jeff began Amazon out of his garage with the financial backing of his parents. At the time, the Internet was still in its infancy, and they never even grasped the concept of this "online bookstore" that he had envisioned. Jeff was honest with them and told them that there was about a 70% chance that they were likely to lose their entire investment. They backed him anyway. Another 50 meetings later, Jeff had managed to raise $1 million as startup capital for his business.

Initially, Jeff drove packages to be posted himself, dreaming of days when the business could expand. By 2001, the business was almost $3 billion in debt. Between the start of the business and the fourth quarter of 2001, the press had a field day with Amazon as a brand, constantly punting it as a failure. Looking back, Bezos will be the first to admit that billions were spent on failures, and that failures come as a result of risk-taking. He also admits that in order to become successful, you must be able to fail and learn something from each of those lessons. According to him, Amazon is the best place to learn to fail.

Two words regarding their business align with his original vision for the business, and that's "Day One." By encouraging everyone within the organization to have a Day One approach to the business, they would simply not have a "failure" mentality.

The main vision of Amazon was to create an organization that was customer-centric. A place where people would keep coming back because of their customer experience. It was never about the product or the books; it was about providing the best possible service available over an e-commerce site (before e-commerce sites were all that popular).

He admits that customer service is something that's challenging to win over and to manage to hold onto, but this has always been the main vision behind the Amazon brand. It was and is, putting the customer first, every single time. Putting the customer first meant innovating ahead of customer needs, and not waiting for them to recommend or ask for additional services to be added into the mix. Amazon managed to do this all on its own, and introduced its Prime membership program. They have also been actively working on speeding up warehousing and delivery times by growing nationally and internationally.

In the early days, Bezos admits that there were threats that Amazon would be swallowed up by other publishing giants, such as Barnes and Noble. Of course, they never felt threatened by Amazon and left him alone. Today, there are many things that set Amazon apart from the rest and it's these things that are the takeaway from his style of leadership:

- Trust is earned slowly

- Do hard things well

- Deliver on time

- Keep promises

- Make tough decisions

- Give customers back time

These are key factors that Bezos has always held at the heart of Amazon. Right now, he shares the spotlight with Elon Musk as the number one ranked business leader in the United States. For him though, it's still about keeping the "Day One" mentality, and this is promoted throughout the organization. The vision he had for Amazon when there were 10 employees, when there were 10,000 employees, 100,000 employees is the same.

As a business, Amazon gives back. Bezos believes in education, in advancing and providing opportunities for those who have been previously disadvantaged. As an organization, they are fully invested in reducing the carbon footprint by ordering 100,000 electric vehicles to be fully operational by 2030. They have invested billions of dollars in their career program, that isn't just limited to studies that will benefit Amazon. Bezos believes that you need to be able to follow your passion. He fully supports the "garage entrepreneurial" spirit, but adds that thanks to the current scale of Amazon, there's so much more that he can do to make a difference and give back. From solar and wind energy, to employing 175,000 new employees over a two-month period during the recent pandemic. The list of ways that Amazon is giving back to the world is almost endless, all because one young man had the vision to bring unprecedented customer service experience to the consumer, ensuring customer loyalty (Bezos, 2020).

Chapter 6: Leadership Qualities / Values

"The challenge of leadership is to be strong, but not rude; be kind, but not weak; be bold, but not bully; be thoughtful, but not lazy; be humble, but not timid; be proud, but not arrogant; have humor, but without folly."

~ Jim Rohn

Leadership Studies

Studies conducted by leadership expert training organization, "Dale Carnegie Training," indicated that, often, expectations that employees have regarding their leaders fall way short.

They specifically list five key areas that need leadership improvement. This study was conducted using more than 3,300 employees globally, with 515 coming from the United States. The study revealed that 84% of workers wanted their leaders to take accountability when they made mistakes, while only 51% of leaders were currently doing so. 88% wanted leaders to really listen to them, while only 61% confirmed that they had leaders who took communication, especially the active listening component of communication, seriously. 86% of those surveyed wanted leaders to recognize them for good work. Only 60% confirmed that this was taking place.

The author of the study wrote that "Employees want leaders who develop themselves and others, making it safe to share their ideas, try new things, make mistakes, learn from them and improve" (Business News Daily Expert Editor, 2016).

Another survey was completed using 5,000 individuals by The Predictive Index to define "what makes a great boss." This indicated that humility, passion, patience, and self-awareness, were the top five skills that most individuals surveyed identified as key characteristics. These traits were necessary for individuals to flourish rather than just get by (Koch, 2019).

The five key attributes that employees were looking for in the Dale Carnegie Training study as reported in Business News Daily, were the following:

Accountability

To be accountable is for leaders to recognize that they are not perfect and have their own set of faults that needed to be managed or overcome, rather than criticizing employees for getting things wrong. 68% of employees were motivated if their leaders indicated that they were also only human and made mistakes from time to time. The ideal way to deal with mistakes as an employee or a leader is to acknowledge that the fault is there, to begin with, to own up to it immediately when a mistake is made (rather than trying to ignore it in the hope that the error will disappear). The next step would be to correct whatever has gone wrong as quickly as possible by coming up with a suitable solution. Often, this means communicating about it and brainstorming suitable solutions to find the best one. For employees, just getting this right was one way that made their leaders more approachable.

Providing Encouragement

This is like the above, yet the shoe is on the other foot and the employee happens to be the one who has made the mistake. 60% of employees would prefer it if their leader gave them the opportunity to correct whatever has been done incorrectly. We've already discussed how important it is to correct someone in private and reward them openly. There's nothing that damages an employer/employee relationship like reprimanding them openly for errors that anyone could have made.

Offering encouragement by recognizing that your employee has improved in an area of their work will take only a moment to do, but can make all the difference in the life of that employee. More than 70% of employees recognized that this should be a vital characteristic for leaders to master to gain respect. As a leader, cast your mind back to when you just started out in the big scary world of work. There were probably many things that you needed to learn before you could really claim competence. This is the same scenario. Your employees don't need to be perfect at something just yet to qualify for encouragement. Recognize that there has been improvement in their work, no matter how small it may seem to you. You will find that your employees will give you a lot more when they are feeling content and happy.

Recognition and Reward

Small tokens of praise and appreciation would go a long way to keep employees motivated and encouraged to give of their best.

75% of leaders miss the boat when it comes to offering their teams small tokens of appreciation or recognition and rewards for doing things well. A large international call center for which I consulted in 2013 used this extremely effectively by gathering their 300+ workforce each Monday morning. The CEO and executive management team would have identified several individuals across the various divisions. They would then be recognized in front of the entire organization. Some of these awards were certificates, cash incentives, or vouchers, product hampers, or promotions within the organization. As a management team, these leaders understood what it meant to keep staff motivated and working towards internal goals and incentives.

On-the-job-Coaching/Training

True leaders arrange for their employees to receive constant encouragement to help them improve within their work. As many as 80% of those surveyed indicated that the best leaders provided learning opportunities for them to develop and grow within the workplace. This doesn't always need to be internal training, coaching, or mentoring. This could also include sending your employees for job-specific training that doesn't only benefit them, but it will benefit the entire organization. It's providing the employee with the best opportunity to be the very best they could be at their job.

The results for leaders who are willing to embrace each of these methods could be extremely positive, not only for themselves as the business leader, but also as far as retention strategies are concerned. Happy employees want to stay and grow within organizations, rather than seeking these qualities from other leaders out there.

Respect from those to whom they report is a major factor, where those who felt as though their leaders respected them, 55% were more engaged in their work than those who never felt secure. Respecting others is more than just saying that you respect them— it's an action. Knowing what your weaknesses through self-awareness make you a better leader.

Honesty/Integrity

Honesty and integrity go hand-in-hand when it comes to leadership and what's required by the workforce to feel as though they can trust you. Employees are quick to pick up on half-truths and (or) lies. It's better to always be honest , rather than bringing up things that are not honest. Part of this is admitting when you're wrong.

Accountability and responsibility may not always be pleasant, but they will help you gain the respect of those you work with and those reporting to you. It's often the little things that we think we can get away with. We tell a little white lie here, and then a little white lie there, feeling confident that each of the lies are small, and there's harm that can come from these small untruths. The problem with lying is that small lies turn into bigger lies, and eventually the lines get so blurred that there's no distinct difference between what's real and what's not.

A leader should be able to stand by whatever they've said and whenever they've said it, because the truth will always remain the same. A lie, on the other hand, is not designed for longevity as the brain is not wired for us to default to an untruth. That's one of the reasons why body language can allow you to easily tell when someone is lying or not. The mind will sift through millions and millions of pieces of information that's stored in your mental mainframe to try and "recall" exactly what you said. There will always be small differences between stories, and when these are each tallied, the lie(s) become easily exposed.

Credibility

Developing credibility as a leader doesn't happen automatically, or overnight. Instead, it takes a fair amount of time for employees to get to know their leaders sufficiently enough to be able to trust them. According to Peter Economy, leadership specialist at Inc., only 49% of employees trust executive leadership. This statistic is high when you consider how many employees feel as though they cannot trust those who lead them daily. What determines whether a leader is credible or not? There are certain characteristics that credible leaders all share. They practice these leadership qualities daily, and this is what sets them apart (Economy, 2015):

- They accept accountability for actions and decisions

- They are experts in their field and can assist coming up with solid working solutions to problems

- They are loyal and display a genuine concern for others

- They are transparent and open and honest in all things

- They can delegate effectively, which builds up trust from those they lead

- They have a strong moral code and align with their ethics

- They look for win-win solutions for all

- They respect others and that respect is reciprocal in return

- They understand that to be able to lead, they need to learn, and that learning is life-long

- They walk-the-walk and talk-the-talk

Motivation

It's one thing being able to motivate yourself and keep yourself going throughout the day, but consistently motivating those reporting to you is something different. Considering this characteristic from the employees' perspective, this is what they need from you as their leader:

- A popular way of becoming motivated in the business through team building events that can boost morale.
- Gaining a perspective from the employee's point of view as another way to motivate them through understanding.
- Involving employees in the decision-making process by teaching them specific areas of the business, motivating them through being taught how the business operates.

Motivation could come from being able to influence individuals towards your way of thinking. It's also helping employees achieve their goals, assisting with personal development in the process.

Motivation is the key to boosting the achievement of personal development goals within an organization that has been identified by the employee.

Rewards and recognition, as we spoke about earlier, could be a way to motivate certain employees, if the rewards are aligned with something the employee feels will be beneficial. Often, this can be as small as a letter of thanks for the work completed. These should be genuine and heartfelt to be effective.

Successful motivation means understanding those reporting to you and what they specifically need individually. One person's needs may be completely different from that of another, and it's your job as a leader to ensure that you can align all these needs with those of the organization.

You can motivate by setting the right example for employees to follow by being an effective role model for them to follow.

Serving

These leaders place their employees first. They understand that being able to collaborate and encourage their team to produce the very best is possible. Results are based on empowerment and upliftment rather than being told what to do all the time. Servant leaders spend time unlocking the creativity and individual potential that may be trapped inside each employee, just waiting to find its way to the surface. This leadership style is where the magic happens, and where employees become more productive because they feel more invested in the organization. Serving is all about the employee, rather than the employer or the leader in the employer's organization.

Awareness

Awareness in leadership could be actual awareness of those who report to them, or awareness of themselves as leaders. Self-awareness is a vital emotional intelligence skill that needs to be tapped into for effective leadership. Authors of *Emotional Intelligence 2.0*, Travis Bradberry and Jean Greaves, state that "83% of people with high self-awareness are top performers ..." (Bradberry & Greaves, 2009).

There are several ways you can boost your self-awareness:

- Are you living true to your belief system, or have you lost your way somehow, getting derailed by the speed at which we live our lives now? Do you feel good about the choices, decisions, and ultimately the path that you're headed towards now? Therefore, self-awareness is so important in leadership. You need to be able to see what's happening in your own life before being able to make changes in the lives of others.

- Ask those you trust for feedback; this might provide some insight into your emotions. Get this feedback from various places, like from colleagues, friends, family members—the broader the input, the more likely you are to get insight that's worthwhile. Having to endure feedback (especially when negative) may be a painful experience, however, it's this feedback that has the greatest value. The feedback received can allow you to see how you communicate with other people.

- Be open to change and adapt along with your team. A great example of this is if you feel most productive towards the end of the day so you always insist on having strategic team meetings during that time. Have you stopped to consider when others are most productive? Have you ever asked? It may mean shifting things around and scheduling these meetings shortly before lunch. You may suddenly receive optimal input from those in your team because you've been prepared to negotiate to meet their needs rather than those of your own.

- Becoming more aware of your feelings, what they mean, and how they're influencing you in the workplace. When you cannot control your own emotions, it's impossible to try and understand the emotions of your team. The best thing to do is to allow your feelings to run their course without holding onto them. Pay attention to the emotions and what they may be trying to teach you. In most instances, there are lessons to be learned from our feelings.

- Get to know yourself better by keeping track of your moods, emotions, and mental and physical states. Keep a journal nearby so that you can write these down. Keep making regular notes without passing judgment or making changes for a couple of months. From there, you will be in a much better place to begin to identify triggers or patterns that cause you to do the things you do. You can also begin to make changes, still tracking each of these in your journal. It's often a healthier sounding board to write your thoughts and emotions down rather than physically lashing out at staff or even at home. It's a great way to recognize personal growth within yourself and coming to terms with areas that need personal growth.

- What are your strengths and weaknesses? Have you asked for feedback from others on this? What you perceive to be strengths or weaknesses may be viewed by others as completely different, especially those under you. Make a list of the feedback you receive so you have a starting point to either further develop (your strengths) or be aware of, as a means of making necessary changes.

- What messages is your body language sending out there? What can you do to change it from being closed and negative, to more open and positive?

Empathy

Empathy is at the very center of being an effective leader. It proves that you have the capacity to be concerned about those you lead. According to Lolly Daskal, author of *The Leadership Gap: What Gets Between You and Your Greatness*, you can use the following ways to improve your skills as an empathetic leader:

- Connect with those you lead by attempting to understanding them better

- Empathy is a core skill necessary for effective leadership

- Empathy strengthens your ability to communicate successfully

- Learn to be more patient with your team

- Pay close attention to those you lead by being in the moment

- Put yourself in their situation before judging them or jumping to conclusions

Empathy is another emotional intelligence skill that can be acquired through extensive practice. It's being able to read the body language and cues that your team are transmitting. Empathy means that you can place yourself in the shoes of those of your team, while seeing things from their perspective rather than your own. It's a humanizing element in leadership. You can show you care about those you lead, without looking soft (Daskal, 2016).

Creativity

Creativity and leadership appear to be at opposite ends of another, however, this has become more and more important for business success. Examples of creative geniuses include individuals such as Steve Jobs, who had a brand-new vision for Apple, Elon Musk, Richard Branson, Mary Barra, and Mark Zuckerberg.

Elon Musk has been prepared to face bankruptcy to get SpaceX off the ground, despite being mocked and ridiculed from those within and outside of his own organization.

Richard Branson has always been about his employees, taking care of them and listening to them. He understands that without his people, there would not be a multi-billion- dollar organization behind the Virgin brand.

Following several deaths due to ignition failures in some of their models, General Motors' newly appointed CEO and Chairman,

Mary Barra, decided to make the biggest recall decision in the history of GM. While she knew that this wasn't likely to score her any popularity points with the GM Board, she also knew it was the right thing to do. This single decision has made her one of the most recognized CEOs in the world today.

Finally, but by no means a lightweight in the creativity department, Mark Zuckerberg only hires on passion rather than skill. It's his belief that skill can be taught, yet passion needs to be part of who the individual is.

Each of these leaders has found creative ways to work through some of their toughest problems. Being prepared to put creativity into action and allowing your employees to come up with creative solutions that your organization may be facing right now. Don't stifle their ideas; they may just surprise you if they're allowed to innovate and think for themselves.

Thoroughness

Being thorough in your work as a leader covers more than just covering certain areas of your job necessary in a monthly or quarterly report. It comes down to having complete knowledge and understanding of all areas of the business. It's knowing exactly what is required of a specific project or goal being managed by the team. In-depth knowledge means that you can break the task down into manageable components which can be delegated to team members, so that targets are met in line with the organization's requirements. Even though delegation takes place, communication of the entire project has also taken place so that everyone is on board with the program.

Taking Risks

Dr. Sharon Porter, CEO of Perfect Time, founder of The GRIND Entrepreneur Network and *Write the Book Now!* explains why taking risks is important for leaders to become successful. She notes that in her early years of teaching, she was fascinated with the autobiographies of successful leaders, and one of the things that she discovered was that there was no specific formula to becoming a great leader. Instead, there were several ways that one could get there. She recalled advice she'd been given once that she claims to be the best single piece advice ever received: "Don't be afraid to take risks" (S H Porter, 2018).

In truth, this is often an area in leadership where we shy away. We look at taking the safe way because taking risks has the element of potential failure attached to it. Part of taking risks should follow a process of getting used to the size of the risks and making certain that they're calculated. Ensure that you have all the information necessary before jumping in brazenly. Much of the time, this means being in tune with your intuition and listening to what it is telling you.

If you're prepared to take risks, you must be prepared to fail forward and ensure that you are able to dissect the results, and discover what went wrong and what you need to change in order to succeed in the future. Taking risks is often going to lead to failure, so you need to be prepared for it. Many leaders take a risk, fail, and then refuse to ever take another risk again because failure feels uncomfortable (which it should). We should always analyze our failures to discover exactly what went wrong and how things might be changed.

Improving

There are several ways that leaders can focus on improving their own leadership skills in such a way that they not only benefit the team, but positively impact the entire organization. Some of these ways are:

Enroll in Leadership Training: There are many leadership training programs available that are often industry-specific. If there are areas you feel you need to improve on, speak with your direct report, or HR, to find out whether or not the organization is prepared to send you for these training courses. If they say no, it's still worthwhile to invest in yourself and do coursework online or after hours. As the market changes, there are more and more reputable organizations offering online courses that can be completed in your own time. Not only will this assist you in the workplace, but it will be another qualification to add to your current portfolio.

Following Those Leaders You Admire: You can follow business leaders who are currently alive online, or study biographies of those reputable leaders who have died. Several leaders immediately spring to mind, such as Steve Jobs, Nelson Mandela, and Stephen Covey. Each of these leaders had different styles, yet were able to get those who followed them to do remarkable things.

Grow Your Network: Business networking is always a great way of improving your own skills. This is simply being able to move in the same circles as great, effective, and successful business leaders. You may be thinking to yourself that you're on the opposite end of the globe from these people; how could you ever make this work? Quite simply, through social networking. Find them on LinkedIn and make sure that you follow their posts, and engage with them in ways that are worthwhile and meaningful. Facebook is a more sociable platform than LinkedIn, so if you want to be taken seriously, ensure that your communications are always professional and applicable.

Remain Transparent: Allow your team to be aware of what you're all about and what you're doing. This goes a long way to garner respect from them, and as you strive to make improvements in your life, they may become motivated to do the same.

Innovation

Innovation and strategic planning go hand-in-hand. Because the world is changing at an ever-increasing pace, companies need to remain innovative and in front of their competitors. Leaders need to remain ahead of trends and changes in the marketplace. This means tracking what is happening or keeping abreast of changes as they're taking place, rather than burying your head in the sand and pretending that all is well. It's knowing that what has worked in the past may not be good enough for the future and admitting that innovative change is necessary to keep ahead of the pack.

As a leader, this could mean being a catalyst for innovative change through teams coming together with solutions that could be implemented to resolve problems. Innovation is more than just coming up with a good idea. It's being able to see the idea through to a result, without becoming distracted. It's also finding workable solutions when problems arise. Most of this is done by collaborating as a team, rather than just leaving it to a single individual.

Chapter 7: Leadership Skills

"The most dangerous leadership myth is that leaders are born-that there is a genetic factor to leadership. That's nonsense; in fact, the opposite is true. Leaders are made rather than born."

~ Warren Bennis

Leaders: Born or Made?

Whether leaders are naturally born to lead, or whether they can learn how to lead is one of the most asked questions about leadership skills. To answer this conundrum, most refer to it as a similar theory as the chicken and the egg, or nature versus nurture. Unpacking this question a bit further, if you are fortunate enough to be born with innate abilities to lead, then it means that conversely, if you weren't fortunate enough to have hit the gene pool jackpot, you're doomed to sit on the sidelines for the rest of your life.

When being asked the same question, career contributor, Erika Anderson from Forbes shares what she's learned through observing thousands of individuals in business over a 30-year period. She indicates that leadership ability can be compared with a bell curve. Some individuals are born with natural leadership abilities. They would find themselves towards the top of the curve. From here, there's only one way for them and that's upwards towards greater leadership. The 10-15% of individuals towards the bottom of the curve would never make effective leaders no matter how many leadership training courses they attend, or how many leadership books they read. Most of these individuals are quite comfortable with who they are and don't aspire to be leaders.

Between these two opposite ends of the spectrum is the largest area of the curve. These individuals have some natural abilities that they are born with, but most of their leadership abilities are learned.

Career and life coach, Erika Anderson, specifies that leaders who are the easiest to coach, train, re-train, and work with are those who are able to place themselves under the microscope and answer the following questions openly and honestly; while we've spoken of strengths and weaknesses in a number of places already, the secret is being able to answer and identify these in your personal life, as well as from a leadership perspective. She suggests asking yourself the following four questions (it will be worthwhile finding a journal that you can reflect in, to use as a benchmark to monitor your growth and development.)

- Are the things you do in line with the commitments you make to others?

- What things are most important to you in your life?

- Do the things you say and do have an impact on those around you? Is this impact a positive or negative one?

- What direction is your moral compass pointing you towards?

Ensure that you check yourself against these four questions regularly to make certain that you are constantly stretching yourself as a leader. With an ever-changing work environment, you may need to reinvent yourself several times throughout your career (Andersen, 2012).

What People Look for In A Leader

While we've already mentioned a lot of qualities that great leaders possess, there are still several people skills and/or characteristics that employees look for in their leaders. Some of these include, but aren't limited to:

Being Effective at Problem-solving

Displaying effective problem-solving abilities means being in a position where you, as a leader, can recognize problems before they arise. The next step would be to manage each problem effectively before it has the chance to do any real damage. Leaders who demonstrate this ability set positive examples for employees so they can identify resources necessary to find solutions.

Creating an Environment That Doesn't Judge Failure

Let's face it, we all fail as we strive to come up with the best possible solutions to challenges. It may mean that you missed a deadline for submitting a report. Failing feels bad enough, and we tend to judge ourselves more harshly than anyone else ever could. When leaders make certain that the environment is a safe space for failure, employees will be motivated to take more calculated risks, learning as they go.

Providing Mentorship and Training

Great leaders learn to recognize the potential in those they lead early on, and are prepared to do something about it. Remember the example of Amazon, with their study fund for employees. The thing that Bezos got right was not limiting further education and not training purely to things that were of benefit to Amazon. Instead, he encouraged employees to follow their dreams and passions.

For those whose passions are aligned with the business, further learning and training through the organization are possible by encouraging mentorship programs. Once in place, it's important to follow through at regular intervals to ensure that the mentor and mentee relationship is working.

Remaining Consistent

It's difficult for employees to get behind a leader who is constantly changing their vision, values, or point of view. Consistency is a vital ingredient for any worthwhile leader who wants to create employees that are prepared to follow them to the ends of the earth. Consistent leaders ensure that their communication is aligned with the vision and mission defined by the company, or the project specific to the team.

Work to Become A Leader People Like

Becoming a leader that people like means more than treating your position as a popularity contest. It's choosing to do things that are often unpopular and uncomfortable, but doing them anyway. Make sure that you're both open to change and new ideas as they come. We know that the business landscape continues to change and evolve almost daily. It's better to develop the attitude of "let's find a way of doing things better together," and then be prepared to change if you must. Be prepared to alter from a fixed mindset of "this is how we've always done it," to a growth mindset of "let's try and solve things using new ideas this time and see how it goes."

Great leaders handle problems as soon as they arise, rather than allowing them to fester and become bigger than they need to be. They understand that when you're working with different personalities, there will always be clashes and commotion no matter how effective they are at leading. Great leaders don't try and stifle these personal differences, instead, they act as facilitators and allow individuals to experience these scenarios for themselves. They don't take sides in these situations; instead, they are both fair and non-judgmental.

Excellent leaders aren't afraid of admitting that there's lots that they don't yet know. They constantly strive towards improvement by making use of every opportunity to learn and grow. They're not afraid of encouraging those they lead to do the same because they understand the value of knowledge. Employees respect these characteristics, and many will even try and model their own behavior on the attributes of a great leader. This opens the door to succession planning that's effective within organizations that have the track record for promoting from within.

Team Building

Team Assessment

Leaders cannot be effective in their day-to-day responsibilities without the support of a good team behind them. So, what defines a good team member? These are ideally individuals who can work both independently and as part of a team. They're driven to achieve the goals set out for them by their leader if it is communicated clearly. Teams should be regularly assessed to make certain that everyone within the team is in the very best position. Leaders should monitor everyone within their team without making them feel as though they're being smothered. If someone happens to be functioning better within another role, don't be afraid to move them into that role (even for a trial period); you never know when someone is going to discover their passion for something they didn't even know they had.

Team assessments can take the form of formal assessments, carried out bi-annually or quarterly. Other assessments can take place on the spot or spur of the moment when the team member least expects it. Assessments are an important way to get to know each member of your team better. It allows you to find out what their hopes and dreams are for the future, and you could even discuss ways to achieve their goals. Happy employees give of their best and remain loyal to the organization.

Motivate Your Team

There are several ways to keep your team motivated and moving in the right direction. One of the most important ways to do so is to lead from the front and lead by example. It's also about being able to act as a cheerleader whenever necessary and provide encouragement from the sidelines. This means still allowing your team to grow and thrive both as individuals and collectively. Ways to motivate your team in the workplace are only limited by your creativity. These could include team-building events, weekend getaways to brainstorm new ideas for a project, introducing different colored clothing for different teams within the organization, inviting guest speakers on a regular basis to boost team morale, or even watching applicable TEDx talks or YouTube videos.

Simple competitions to motivate towards project completion could help you reach tight deadlines. Regular awards or rewards could be offered as part of an incentive program like the international call center I mentioned earlier on. Whatever you decide to do, you will find your employees becoming a lot more engaged in the work process.

> <u>*As a sidebar*</u>: *It's not about the value or price tag attached to the reward that counts, as much as the team-based incentive. You are looking at creating an environment that is filled with positive and healthy competition. What's most important is that you, as the leader, follow through with whatever you promise.*

Empower Your Team

One of the best ways to empower your team is by stepping back, releasing the reins, and allowing those on your team to take control of themselves. This will often be a great way to measure performance, supervisory skills, and many other attributes that team members might possess. If you're too close to the situation, it's easy to overlook these positive characteristics, or for them to get lost in the day-to-day functioning of the business.

An important part of empowering your team is allowing them to fail, knowing that you will still be there as a means of support. Those who have experienced failures or setbacks should be encouraged to continue in their efforts. It's important for leaders to reassure these individuals that failure is part of growing, and help them identify the lesson to be learned.

Provide Job-Specific Training

Great leaders ensure that their team members know exactly what's required of them and by when. If they're in need of any job-related training, it's part of your responsibility to ensure that this happens. It is also up to you to ensure that they have whatever tools are needed for them to be able to fulfill their work obligation to the organization. This could mean specialty software to be able to be effective, or other office equipment. Deadlines can depend on a multitude of things, from knowledge-based operations to technical support, due to faulty equipment. As the leader of any team, it should be your responsibility to ensure that the wheels are kept in motion, moving the work of the organization forward.

Lead Teams

Teams often need direction, and good leaders can lead in all directions. This means that they're effective in leading from the top downwards, from the bottom upwards, and able to lead effectively sideways. They can organize teams according to their specific strengths for optimum value of each individual team member. It's all about understanding how to maximize these strengths by planning work strategically, rather than flying by the seat of your pants.

Not all teams have strong individuals who are prepared to step out of the shadows and take the lead when necessary, and it's at times like these when leaders need to be specifically cognizant of this. When this happens, it may be worthwhile appointing someone to take control of the project and be responsible for reporting back on progress. That way, you are gently assisting them to take on new responsibilities, teaching them how to delegate and communicate; and while they may not realize it at the time, you're forcing them out of their comfort zone.

Encourage Loyalty

One of the largest challenges in business today is how to gain loyalty from your employees without forcing it upon them. Loyalty today is way different than in the past, when the silent generation or baby boomers were the majority in the workplace.

The business model has completely changed with Generation-X, Millennials, GenY, and even some GenZ replacing these stalwarts of society. Each of these new generations has completely different ways of working, and according to the Gallup Business Journal, the statistics from a recent survey on Millennials tell the whole story:

- They are the generation that's most likely to change jobs

- 60% confirm that they are open to considering other opportunities

- Most millennials have totally zoned out of their current jobs

Therefore, coming up with solid retention strategies is vitally important for the modern leader. And, it's just as important to ignite a flame of passion within this generation to keep them active and engaged in the workplace. Without it, although they turn up for work, they already have one foot out of the door (Gallup Business Journal, n.d.).

Retention Strategies

High staff turnover is one of the largest challenges facing organizations and leaders over the last decade or so. As Millennials take over and become the single largest working group in the U.S. at present, controlling what HR professionals, hiring managers, and recruiters refer to as the "churn" of staff is their single biggest human resource challenge. Rehiring quality replacements often cost organizations double the previous incumbent's salary and then there is an expenditure that are seldom calculated:

- Retraining of a new hire

- Loss of proprietary information with ex-employee

- Client frustration waiting for replacement employees to learn your way of doing things

- Ability to work as a cohesive team once trusted has been re-established

It's much better to have a firm retention strategy in place, with ways to retain top talent within your organization, than having to replace them once they leave. This can include anything from competitive salaries to offering flexibility regarding where they operate. Remote work is becoming more in demand now than ever before, as Millennials make lifestyle choices rather than being chained to a desk in a small cubicle. They want the freedom to make their own decisions. Once you have their buy-in, they will be loyal to your organization and give you their very best work.

Vision

According to Kristi Hedges, executive coach, leadership development consultant, speaker, and author of *The Power of Presence* and *The Inspiration Code*, she confirms that becoming an effective and efficient leader takes time. It's not something that you suddenly decide to do by waking up in the morning. It takes time, effort, and practice. There are likely to be many times when you fail before your team, and those responsible for you will begin to accept and follow your vision for the future (Hedges, 2018).

Vision is where it all starts. We've often heard that organizations have their own mission statements and vision of where they would like to see the organization go. As a smaller division of a major multinational organization, it's vital that your divisional goals and vision align with the greater, overall vision and mission as the backbone to whatever you collectively decide is right for your division. The following are some key criteria when it comes to developing the right kind of vision within an organization—the vision that employees will follow:

Everyone Has a Role to Play

Ensure that everyone knows what the vision is, how it connects back to the overall vision of the company or organization, and what specific roles each member of the team needs to play. Inclusion is important to secure buy-in from those who are uncertain whether or not they should be following two sets of directions. One as outlined by the organization's senior executive committee, and the other that's closely aligned with where the division or department needs to be moving towards. Like a well-oiled machine, everyone within the division has a vital role to play towards the achievement of divisional goals.

Faces Toward the Future

There's no point in deciding on visions or goals that are not going to propel you towards future achievement. You aren't looking to stagnate, but rather, want to encourage the members of your team to strive to be better and do better every single day. If you can encourage them to be even a fraction better today than what they were yesterday, imagine the impetus this could have on moving your team towards the right trajectory.

Inspires Followers

While it's often said (and I paraphrase) that "great leaders are supposed to create other great leaders", I would reason that the world would be unable to function effectively if there were only great leaders. There need to be followers too. Great leaders have the capacity to inspire their followers to achieve whatever it is that they've set their sights on. This could be anything from meeting specific project deadlines to meeting sales budgets. These leaders can monitor the temperature of the team, even from a distance, and continue to motivate them. This motivation needs to occur daily—even on those days when you, as a leader, simply feel like giving in and allowing someone else to take over for a while. It's on days like these that you need to drag yourself out of bed, put your best face on (even if it is a façade for the day), and remain positive for those who are following you into the business fray daily.

Keep it Visible

Your mission statement (as agreed upon with all involved parties) needs to remain visible for everyone. This may necessitate some out-of-the box thinking. Whether this means making a large enough sign that everyone has to pass several times a day, or something smaller that contains the vision statement that can be at each desk within the department, find a way for your people to be able to internalize this mission and goals. It should be able to inspire them towards greater achievement daily. Having to stare at a mission statement daily, or reading it daily, will ensure that it becomes part of the very fiber of everyone in the team. It will help them internalize the ethos behind the mission that you're trying to achieve as a collective group of individuals.

Maps External Terrain

This is one of the most important roles when working with mission statements at the divisional or departmental level. The idea is that the major, overarching mission of the organization features in your departmental vision somehow. As the leader of these individuals, it's your responsibility to help your team connect the dots between the global organizational vision and the departmental vision.

A real-life example of this was when Mary Barra, the CEO and Chairman of General Motors was still heading up the Global HR Division. Her vision was to reduce the size of the corporate dress code manual which was over 20+ pages in length. So how did she do it? She addressed the various divisions and passed the responsibility onto them, holding each employee accountable. She reminded leaders that they were responsible for hundreds of staff members, and budgets that ran into hundreds of thousands of dollars, if not more. If they were able to be trusted with people and money, surely, she should be able to trust them with how to dress. The new dress code manual (section), reads: "dress appropriately".

Chapter 8: Leadership Dysfunctions

"Not finance. Not strategy. Not technology. It is teamwork that remains the ultimate competitive advantage, both because it is so powerful and so rare."

~ Patrick Lencioni

According to Ozgur Savas and his study entitled *Impact of Dysfunctional Leadership on Organizational Performance,* as published in the Global Journal of Management and Business Research: Administration and Management, he says that everyone is so focused on reporting and printing about the positive characteristics of leaders, that nobody ever discusses those that are toxic or dysfunctional. Unfortunately, despite how little is written about it, the reality is that dysfunctional leaders both exist and can seriously impact a team negatively (Savas, 2019).

Various negative leaders have been given some of the following titles and we will discuss each of these briefly, as well as identify other ways that dysfunction can creep into the workplace. First up, there are several dysfunctional names awarded to those leaders who create havoc in their wake.

Abusive Leadership

Abusive leadership can be any form of leadership, management, or supervision where the leader is perceived to be abusive in the workplace. This abuse could be anything from constant verbal-abuse or aggressive behavior. Abuse could also be tearing employees apart in public (we discussed rewarding in public and criticizing in private), and this type of leader would get a kick out of creating public humiliation for employees. Part of the problem with abusive leadership is whether it's happening, or whether it's a perception on the part of the employee.

Advantages of Abusive Leadership

There has been some empirical research done to determine whether there are actual advantages to abusive leadership. These have identified a couple of areas that may be construed as positive and advantageous to employees:

Should there be a large enough gap between the leader and the "abused" employee, it may just spur them on to furthering studies to place them in line for a promotion. The same study mentioned that should these employees be reprimanded for making a mistake, they would be less likely to repeat the same mistake again (Zhu & Zhang, 2019).

Authoritarian Leadership

Examples of authoritarian leadership would be any of the dictators as recorded in history, such as Julius Caesar in ancient Rome, Fidel Castro from Cuba, Adolf Hitler from Germany, Robert Mugabe from Zimbabwe, and many others. This is not to say that authoritarian leadership is strictly linked to politics, because it isn't. This type of leader is only concerned about themselves, and what's in it for them. Although they are still responsible for teams, they seldom take the time to consult with them when decisions need to be made. Instead, they follow their own set of rules and guidelines.

Disadvantages of Authoritarian Leadership

Constant criticism from this type of leader reduces the overall morale of the team.

The skills of the group are limited to the skills of the leader. If team members are more qualified or experienced than the leader, this won't have any positive influence because the leader will constantly block them with their "I know best," attitude.

There is no room for growth under this style of leadership, which can frustrate employees, often leading employees to seek opportunities elsewhere.

This leader points out mistakes the moment they happen, and feedback is mainly negative.

This leader stifles innovation and creativity within teams. This can also frustrate employees and lead to staff turnover.

Machiavellian Leadership

This type of leadership is named after Italian born bureaucrat, Niccolo Machiavellian, who happened to write a "leadership" book titled *The Prince* in 1513. The book was filled with ways to manipulate others to do your bidding, or to conform to your way of thinking. By 1970, this leadership style was labeled as being hostile, toxic, and manipulative. For most Machiavellian leaders, it's about being able to control those reporting to them through whatever means necessary, including fear tactics, wielding power, open retaliation, and embarrassment of those beneath them. Machiavellians can also display narcissistic tendencies and cannot deal with failure. They are hostile, arrogant, and demanding of attention as they crave success.

The main problem with this style of leadership is that it leads to toxicity within an organization and irrational decision-making. They have no moral compass whatsoever, but demand being respected by others (even when they're clearly undeserving of this honor). When things don't go as planned, these individuals are the ones that will be first in line throwing temper-tantrums, finger-pointing always outward. They don't accept responsibility for failure or error. It's always as a result of someone else and never themselves. These leaders have the potential to destroy entire organizations (Schaeffer, 2018).

Narcissistic Leadership

How can you tell if you're working for a narcissistic leader? And what can you do about it? Marriage counselor and life/career coach, Kathy Caprino confirms several ways to identify these destructive individuals. Kathy worked as an attorney for a few blue-chip organizations, hating every moment of it, until she discovered her actual passion was still helping people, but as a coach, instead of appearing in a courtroom. During her tenure with these large organizations, she tells of many experiences working for and alongside narcissists and how destructive they can be (Caprino, 2011).

Some of their characteristics are that:

- Narcissists have mastered the art of lying (even to the point where you're certain they believe their own lies).

- Their most dangerous characteristic is the inability to challenge them—ever! This is where their power kicks in, and before you even know what's hit you, you'll have a box with all the little goodies from your desk in a box, marching towards the EXIT sign.

- They are completely unfeeling and can neither sympathize nor empathize with their team.

- They are rule-breakers unless the rules are made by them, and even then, it would only be as the rules were in their favor.

- They can create high-energy environments in the workplace purely based on their high degree of enthusiasm.

- They like to be surrounded by people who adore them.

- While they come across all charming in daylight, beware of the sting in the scorpion's tail.

Unpredictable Leadership

The unpredictable leader lives up to their name, blowing hot one moment and cold the next. Being efficient and effective as a team member reporting to an unpredictable leader can be frustrating. The amount of time and energy that goes into trying to determine what they want next creates an environment where there is plenty of lagging, and little genuine progress in being able to move forward. If you are this type of leader, you need to come to terms with the fact that you're not "keeping your staff on their toes," by being unpredictable. You are setting the team up for frustration and failure. The main frustration comes as they're scrambling to predict your next move, instead of being able to synchronize with you.

The ideal working environment should have a leader that creates harmony and a cohesive unit, all working towards a common goal, rather than part of a dysfunctional team.

Management Skills

We have covered a lot of management skills that crossover as leadership skills as well. With honesty and integrity, for leaders it's important not just to be yelling and telling employees what to do. They need to hold themselves accountable to the same set of standards.

Decision-making in Leadership

Before diving into specific types of decision-making in leadership, what's most important of all is that decisions are made. It can be said that making a bad decision is better than no decision. Indecision in itself is already a decision that's been made. Successful leaders go from decision to decision as quickly as possible. Even if the decision that they've made doesn't pan out, they are able to change course and move in another direction with their team backing them up all the way.

Lean Management

Lean decision-making in a management context is a means to cut out delays in the decision-making process, which is experienced in virtually every organization globally. Managers and leaders are faced with multiple challenges, problems, or even conventional decisions that need to be made every single day. By implementing a Lean decision-making approach, organizations are able to make decisions a lot quicker than they normally would have. Decisions are also spread throughout the workforce, ending the finger-pointing blame game.

Lean decision-making happens when several staff members are empowered with decision-making for and on behalf of the organization, or as part of a specific project. Because the decision is made collectively, no single individual can be held responsible should the decision be the incorrect one. The team is empowered with the ability to course-correct should the decision be incorrect, and they're encouraged to base all decisions on as many facts, figures, and information that they can possibly acquire. With Lean decision-making, it's encouraged to leave decisions for as long as possible, while data and information are collected. This would result in the decision being based on as many facts and evidence to support the decision as possible.

Lean decision-making has been proven to be more transparent, predictable, and positive than when systems were not present (Simons et al., 2016).

Problem Solving

One of the biggest challenges when it comes to problem-solving in leadership is that you get some leaders who are extremely good at it. To the point where they can immediately pick up that there's a problem, they can trace the problem back to its root cause and they're able to resolve it in hardly any time at all. You may be asking why this type of skill could present a challenge for leaders? In truth, if a leader can analyze, diagnose, and repair rapidly on their own, what's the point of being surrounded by a team? Apart from this, how is any member of this leader's team meant to learn and grow on their own? Learning is acquired from physically doing, which means that for team members to grow into effective leaders themselves, they must begin somewhere. They need to learn and to grow through shared experiences. You, as their leader with exceptional problem-solving abilities, can make use of this exceptional teaching moment to share these skills with those who would like to learn how. Of course, the scale and scope of every single problem are likely to be different and unique. This is what makes it so exciting for your team members.

For some, it will take a deep-dive analysis of the problem. For others, it may need in-depth research into the mechanics of how something works.

One of your key responsibilities as a leader is to solve problems effectively. The strange thing about having to deal with problems is that they seem to be never-ending, and you no sooner deal with one and another one starts. According to a high-performance leadership coach, Glenn Llopis, it's not really the problem that's the problem; it's not having enough time to deal with the problem effectively from the start. He suggests the following four ways that leaders use to solve problems (Llopis, 2013).

Communication needs to be transparent with everyone involved on the various levels feeling as though they are free to engage in open dialogue as part of a team.

Following through with transparent communication comes the breaking down of divisional or individualized silos that people, departments, or organizations place themselves in. It's being able to identify where each staff member belongs, and enabling them with a free, safe space in which to operate.

The third step, according to Llopis, is for individuals to be open-minded so that the road to change and problem-solving can be as short and unencumbered as possible. Individuals who are open-minded aren't afraid to take risks and because of this, problems are solved much quicker than under normal circumstances.

The final step is strategic change. It's not good enough in problem-solving to substitute or stick a band-aid over it. Instead, genuine problem-solving requires radical change, improvement, and replacement. This replacement may be anything from policies and procedures to physical equipment to resolve recurring issues (Llopis, 2013).

Where problems are concerned in organizations, they will always be there, although no two problems are likely to ever be the same. Effective leaders can take charge in these situations, no matter how uncomfortable or unpleasant they may be. They are prepared to make some tough decisions and calls if that's what's necessary to fix what may be currently broken.

Process Improvement

Every organization and department run on a specific set of rules and guidelines, often referred to as policies and procedures. Even within a manufacturing environment, there are specific tasks or process flows that need to happen one after another. It would be impossible for an accountant to do the books for two months in advance when (s)he doesn't have any viable data to be working from.

Process improvement is being able to optimize specific organizational tasks, structures, policies, procedures, or processes to make the organization operate at its optimum capacity or level of efficiency. As a leader, it's your responsibility to ensure that your division is running at its best. Some of the ways to achieve this are to closely analyze the area you've either identified as having a problem, or the division you may want to optimize. One of the best ways I've discovered is by paying close attention to process flow just by quietly watching how things are handled. Is there somewhere that the business "flow" appears to hit a snag or a bottleneck? If so, how can this be rectified? For process improvement to be successful, you need complete transparency. If you know that your department is always on their best behavior when you're around, hire an external third-party that poses absolutely no threat to them whatsoever.

It's easy for those reporting to you to open to a neutral third party. Even running blind or anonymous questionnaires could prove valuable when you're either looking for a cause for inefficiency. As a strong leader, should change be necessary, it should be managed effectively in- house by yourself. This is where things can become uncomfortable, especially if tough decisions need to be made. What's most important, however, is that everything that happens should be in the best interest of both the organization and employees. The more win-win's you're able to notch up, the more your team will want to collaborate and work with you on making things better for all.

Crisis Handling and Conflict Resolution

Identify Good & Bad Conflicts

This is almost like addressing the elephant in the room in the workplace, yet it's one of the topics that most leaders shy away from. Unfortunately, whether you like it or not, crisis handling and conflict resolution are part of your role as a leader. It's your job to be dealing with it and rather than trying to avoid it, the best thing to do is to engage and minimize the fallout as quickly as possible.

Whether we'd care to admit it or not, we are all social beings, and each one of us is different. There are many individuals in the workplace who are out for blood and whose sole purpose or adrenaline rush for the day comes from the creation of sheer chaos, mayhem, and havoc. These individuals will do anything to manipulate those around them as best they can. As a leader, it's your job to recognize what is happening as quickly as possible, and to handle each of these situations with as much grace and ease as you possibly can.

Leaders should be unbiased and fair whenever it comes to conflict resolution. This means not picking sides from the get-go, and being prepared to consider all sides from every angle. While conflict resolution comes along with every job in every industry, it's best to not let it fester. Instead, seek amicable solutions that are fair to all parties concerned. I'm not advocating for one moment that an individual should prove to be more guilty of a serious offense that carries higher penalties and be treated less harshly. In fact, this is part of being a leader—making the tough calls whenever necessary. For example, if someone is guilty of corporate espionage, you're not going to hold the door open for them to leave with all your proprietary information. Instead, you are going to follow all the correct legal channels to ensure your organization is protected.

However, if they are being set up by someone else and this comes to light during your investigation, the act of slander and false accusations should also not be tolerated in the workplace. Remember that you're all spending most of your time at the workplace, so you should at least make it somewhere that people want to be. Very few people do drama very well in our fast-paced society. Make certain that employees and colleagues like and trust you. As they do so, you will be amazed at how much more you are able to get out of them than what they are currently doing.

Chapter 9: Leadership

Communication

"Communication is a skill that you can learn. It's like riding a bicycle or typing. If you're willing to work at it, you can rapidly improve the quality of every part of your life."

~ Brian Tracy

Communicate Effectively

Without optimal, effective communication in leadership, no organization can thrive in modern society. As a leader especially, because you're responsible for so many diverse teams and individuals, communication could easily become a slippery slope. There's also a whole lot more to communication than sending out emails to those reporting to you or barking orders. According to the Center for Creative Leadership, "effective leadership and effective communication are intertwined."

Effective communication is being able to communicate successfully with a diverse group of people as individuals. No two people are the same, and it would be foolish to think that the way you communicate with one person would necessarily work in the same way when communicating with the next. Apart from this, there are subtle, yet distinct, differences between the way that you would communicate with your board of directors or a key client, and your team during a social event.

Have you ever considered that the way you communicate may be the reason why people either do what you want them to do or completely ignore your request, moving in the opposite direction? To become more effective in your communication with those around you, means understanding each of them individually, rather than collectively. When it comes to corporate communication and business leadership, this is one of the key areas that break-down (Center for Creative Leadership Blog, 2019).

Optimize Your Communication

Mastering the art of communication is a sure-fire way to improve your leadership skills and genuinely connect with your team. Leadership guru, John C. Maxwell, in his bestseller, *Everyone Communicates Few Connect: What the Most Effective People Do Differently*, redefines this "connection" in five categories, briefly summarized as (Maxwell, 2010):

Finding Common Ground

This is his first and most important rule in being able to connect with those around you, no matter the reason. Be aware that you need to see things from others' viewpoints, rather than your own. According to Maxwell, "It's difficult to find common ground with others when the only person you're focused on is yourself" (Maxwell, 2010).

Keeping Your Communication Simple

The world of communication is complex enough as it is at the moment, where almost everyone is trying to sound better educated and more knowledgeable than the next. While this may be necessary if you are writing for technical publications or academic papers, it's not necessary in the world of business. The best advice that I've ever received was from one of my editors when they indicated that every word should count, rather than writing towards the word count. Communication should be clear and straightforward so that your message cannot be misinterpreted. For this simple communication approach to work, Maxwell introduces a five-step strategy (Maxwell, 2010):

1. Get to the point as quickly as possible.

2. Repeat yourself three times so things are heard, recognized, and finally learned. This is how we each learn, through repetition and understanding.

3. Communicate clearly and simply so that even a child can understand what you're trying to say.

4. Saying less is often saying more, especially when you're trying to get a very specific message across.

5. Talk to people and not above them. Even though you are the leader, you don't need to communicate with your team as though they are too dumb to understand.

This involves being able to be interesting to others, and what interests you is not always it. It's having those you're working with, speaking to, writing to, or addressing to be interested in what you have to say because it's done in such a way that it captures their interest and attention. Whatever medium you choose to use, the language and examples should reflect the target audience, and not always your own personal belief system.

Inspiring People Through Communication

Whether we realize it or not, we are communicating with those around us throughout the day. Some of this communication is verbal, while much of it is non-verbal. It's all the things that we don't actually say, but our face gets to say it, or body language gives it away. These skills form part of the self-awareness that we discussed earlier. They are also emotional intelligence attributes. You need to be self-aware of all the ways that you may be communicating your genuine emotions without meaning to.

Be specifically attentive to your body language. Open up, or make sure that during meetings you're not sending defensive signals to things people are saying. Watch out for folding your arms or crossing your legs, making your personal space smaller than it needs to be. Become the kind of communicator that people leave a meeting with the attitude, "that was really worthwhile, I got a lot out of it," rather than, "just another boring old meeting, nothing ever really happens. What a waste of time." (I'm sure that you've attended more than enough of these!)

Discovering the secret to inspiring those you lead really depends on the dynamics of your team. Some teams work well with morning meetings where they can air their opinions openly and discuss what needs to be achieved during the day. Others respond better to written communications in the form of individual, group, or team emails that are more specific and motivating at the same time. The main aim of this type of communication, whether verbal or non-verbal, face-to-face, or written, is that it achieves the objective of being able to motivate those in your team.

Staying Authentic in All Your Relationships

In his final tip, Maxwell indicates that the buy-in to a change in leadership within an organization and all the hype that goes along with it, usually only lasts for an average of six months. By that time, the leader would have had to have cemented their credibility that they are as genuine as they originally intended to be. They would have had to display that they are the type of leader they communicated they were. He refers to this as the "honeymoon being over" (Maxwell 2010). By this time, employees would have quickly identified whether the leader is authentic and trustworthy, that their word is their bond, or not.

Part of being authentic in relationships is not talking "down" to employees and then switching it up with your superiors. This is just fake, and your employees will pick this up really quickly. Don't try to be different from one group of people. Rather, stay true to your authentic self at all times.

Improve Your Communication Skills

Be an Active Listener. This is one of the most challenging areas for me personally, and I'm sure that I'm not alone. I really need to concentrate and be aligned with the individuals I am communicating with, and this involves physically being way more attentive to what they are saying verbally, as well as what they are saying non-verbally. What is their body language telling me? Am I listening with half an ear because I'm already trying to come up with the best solution to their concerns (when they haven't even finished voicing their concerns entirely yet)? Is it more important for me to hear my own voice rather than allowing the voices of my team to be heard, whether individually or collectively?

Be Professional, Rather Than a Comedian

This speaks to how well you know and interact with your audience. It's also important to understand that while you can be lighthearted some of the time during dialogue, passing on vital corporate information should not be done tongue-in-cheek, or in a way where the audience may consider the message to be a joke. It's more important to earn the respect of those with whom you're communicating than getting a laugh.

Beware of Body Language

Whether we care for the statistics or not, studies (Yaffe, 2011) have indicated that around 55 percent of how and what we communicate is nonverbal. This is done through a series of nonverbal cues and through our mannerisms. Most of the time, we aren't even aware that we have folded our arms, crossed our legs in a certain way, or chosen to make ourselves look like the shrinking violet in the room.

Communicate Key Points Effectively

Start and end your presentation by introducing what you plan to discuss in the meeting. Highlight each of these key points so they are clearly understood. By the end of your meeting, each of the key points discussed should be summarized to ensure the audience has understood what was discussed. This is an extremely effective method of communicating during meetings. The entire goal of this type of communication is to ensure that the audience is taking the right message away with them.

Encourage Audience Participation

The worst possible meetings are where one individual stands and does all the talking, while everyone else in the room becomes totally disengaged from what's happening. You can recognize that this is happening the moment individuals begin looking at their watches, the clock on the wall, checking their phones, doodling on paper they've brought with them etc. By asking important questions, you should be able to keep the attention of those in the room. You can be specific by addressing certain questions directly to one individual, asking for their take or feedback on the situation. Generally, the bored, glazed over look will only happen once if you take this advice. Others within the team will want to be prepared if they are called upon in the next meeting.

Make Sure Your Message Is Understood

Too often, we take for granted that people will understand exactly what we are trying to say, and will get the message right the first time, every time. This assumption is way off the mark. In order to understand things correctly, we need to repeat the same message several times. It's also worthwhile having the "audience" respond by letting you know what they perceived the message to be. This way, should there be any confusion, it can be clarified immediately.

Make Use of Technology Only When Necessary

While we have mentioned that PowerPoint should not be used as a medium for meetings, if you are likely to be giving the same presentation over and over again, it may be worthwhile to record it on platforms such as Zoom or Wistia. Each of these platforms allows the user to edit videos so they are at their best before being posted. These videos could be especially helpful when onboarding new employees.

Reduce Visual Aids

This relates to things like PowerPoint presentations. Avoid these at all costs. Both Steve Jobs, the late Apple CEO, and Sheryl Sandberg from Facebook, eliminated the use of this medium within their organization as they discovered that they are not as helpful in getting the message across to individuals. Within each of these multi-billion-dollar industries, leaders have been encouraged to use their words, rather than relying on technology.

Request Feedback

One of the best ways to improve your communication skills is by asking for honest feedback from your colleagues, peers, and team members on a regular basis. We are often too close to a situation to recognize when there is a problem. Ensure that feedback is open and honest, even if you need to draw up a questionnaire that has relevant questions regarding the way you communicate that can be submitted anonymously.

Speak from The Heart

Another word for this type of communication is 'extemporaneous'. This is where you can write down several key points that you want to cover, yet you have not necessarily written out an entire scripted speech. This type of document allows you to communicate effectively by covering all the thoughts and ideas that you wanted to get across, while, at the same time, not being tethered to a formal speech where you read it verbatim. It allows you some creative latitude, and the speech doesn't come across as being rigid or forced.

Conclusion

"No man will make a great leader who wants to do it all himself, or to get all the credit for doing it."

~ Andrew Carnegie

Leadership in the 21st century is anything from straightforward and black and white. There are thousands of shades of grey that different organizations utilize to attempt to keep ahead of the pack or to inch out their competition. While the previous chapters have been as in-depth as possible, there is always much to be learned from other leadership experts, particularly those that are industry-specific.

Look to the past without becoming stuck there, for there are many lessons to be learned from many of the great leadership experts such as Napoleon Hill, Dale Carnegie, Jack Welch, and other giants of the old industry. Today, there are new leaders to mold and shape your career around. Look to each of these leaders for encouragement and guidance. Every conceivable industry has an iconic leader that is currently blazing a trail into the future. Find one that appeals to you, and study what they have done to make themselves who they are today.

Getting the basics right when it comes to leadership is the necessary first step. It's deciding the kind of leader that you'd like to be and then learning how to master each of the skills and characteristics of these leaders. In my humble opinion, servant-based leadership and situational-leadership suit my personal needs best. Remember that you can learn and develop those leadership characteristics you don't believe you currently possess. Although there are certain natural characteristics closely aligned with leadership that you could be born with, such as being able to convince others to follow you or having excellent communication skills, for most leaders, they need to discover many of these traits themselves.

In *Leadership 2.0,* you have each of these key characteristics and skills neatly laid out over each of the nine chapters where there are pearls of wisdom tucked away in each one. As promised, data substantiate each of the claims made, and statistics have been quoted. The information has been carefully researched and backed by empirical data to support each claim.

Strive to become an extraordinary leader by doing things differently. Identify the leadership style that works best for you and those around you. If you have a team that's mixed with a rich diversity of individuals, then situational leadership may be the best route to consider. Rather than settling for one style, you may need to switch it up depending on the conditions you're being faced with at the time. This may result in micro-managing certain individuals on your team during specific projects, whilst encouraging creative freedom from them at other times. This is how to master situational leadership. It requires flexibility and your willingness to change your style of leadership as often as required.

Remember that although certain leadership characteristics are potentially innate (meaning you're born with them), most of these skills can be learned and mastered over time. The key takeaway from this section is that you need to be consistent, no matter what. Individuals who battle to come to terms with the direction they should be heading in themselves cannot expect to be effectual leaders. Your path and direction should be so deeply ingrained in your mind that you ignite and display the passion of a great leader that individuals want to follow. Do the things that great leaders do by developing effective leadership habits. These begin with your daily habits. How you begin your day will set the tone for not only you, but for the rest of your team. Your mood when you're in the workplace will directly impact those around you. As a leader, it's best to leave any personal upheavals at the door. When your team sees you focused on what needs to be done, they will mirror your behavior.

The key to process improvement is constantly trying to reinvent yourself as a leader. A while back, there was a challenge on Facebook to maintain health and well-being during lockdown by doing push-ups. The goal was to start small, and add just a single additional push-up each day. This same process can be applied to leadership. You don't need to get it 100% right the first time. I know that I most certainly didn't. The goal is to see small, incremental improvements every day. Set yourself small, manageable goals that you know you can achieve. Like the single push-up, adjust the goal upwards slightly until eventually, you've mastered the area you wanted to improve.

With leadership comes the importance of managing yourself and who you are as a leader. This means being acutely aware of what you do and say. The most key takeaway when it comes to communication is that it's not always verbal. Our faces often say more than we'd like them to through micro-cues. These can be little things we're doing subconsciously. It's rolling our eyes at a comment we don't agree with, or raising an eyebrow, or moving your mouth in a certain direction. Add this to your arsenal of strategic ammunition regarding communication with others.

The single most important takeaway is that you need to discover your true authentic self as a leader and then work fiercely, passionately, and fearlessly to become the very best leader you have the potential to be. You now have the tools in your hands and at your disposal; what you choose to do with this information is completely up to you. You could use it to become the very best version of yourself you can be. Become the type of leader that others would want to follow, that they'd choose to look up to and emulate. Because leadership is constantly changing, you have the perfect opportunity to make yourself into whatever type of leader you'd like to be.

I hope that you will refer to this volume often, that each of the headings will inspire you, or provide you with relevant information that you need on your leadership journey in the 21st century. Remember that you have the potential for greatness, you just need to want it bad enough. Once you do, go after it with everything that you have, and a little bit extra for good measure.

Reach for your dreams in this brand new leadership landscape; it can be anything you want it to be!

Peter Allen

Premium Content

Subscribe to our receive premium content on productive meetings, business success, marketing mastery, sales conversion, team management and much more

https://www.subscribepage.com/premiumcontent

Access

References

Adkins, A. (2016, May 12). *Millennials: The job-hopping generation.* Gallup.Com; Gallup. https://www.gallup.com/workplace/231587/millennials-job-hopping-generation.aspx

admin. (2015, May 11). *My top 10 quotes on communication.* Virgin. https://www.virgin.com/richard-branson/my-top-10-quotes-communication

Andersen, E. (2012, December 16). Are leaders born or made? *Forbes.* https://www.forbes.com/sites/erikaandersen/2012/11/21/are-leaders-born-or-made/

Anthony, L. (2019). *Define situational leadership.* Chron.Com. https://smallbusiness.chron.com/define-situational-leadership-2976.html

Appian. (2017). *What is process improvement? | Appian.* Appian.Com. https://www.appian.com/bpm/process-improvement-organizational-development/

Bezos, J. (2020, July 28). *Statement by Jeff Bezos to the U.S. house committee on the judiciary.* US Day One Blog. https://blog.aboutamazon.com/policy/statement-by-jeff-bezos-to-the-u-s-house-committee-on-the-judiciary

Boiser, L. (2019, June 27). *End employee blame games with lean decision-making.* Kanban Zone. https://kanbanzone.com/2019/end-blame-games-lean-decision-making/

Bradberry, T., & Greaves, J. (2009). *Emotional intelligence 2.0.* Talentsmart.

Business News Daily Expert Editor. (2016). *5 Traits employees want in a boss.* Business News Daily.

https://www.businessnewsdaily.com/9584-best-boss-traits.html

Caprino, K. (2011, December 12). *How to tell if your boss is a narcissist-- And 5 ways to avoid getting fired by one.* Forbes. https://www.forbes.com/sites/kathycaprino/2011/12/12/how-to-tell-if-your-boss-is-a-narcissist-and-5-ways-to-avoid-getting-fired-by-one/#5a1687ace08

Caprino, K. (2019, July 7). *Narcissistic leaders—the destructive lies they tell themselves and others.* Forbes. https://www.forbes.com/sites/kathycaprino/2019/06/07/narcissistic-leadersthe-destructive-lies-they-tell-themselves-and-others/

Center for Creative Leadership Articles. (n.d.-a). *Giving thanks will make you a better leader.* Center for Creative Leadership. https://www.ccl.org/articles/leading-effectively-articles/giving-thanks-will-make-you-a-better-leader/

Center for Creative Leadership Articles. (n.d.-b). *The importance of empathy in the workplace.* Center for Creative Leadership. https://www.ccl.org/articles/leading-effectively-articles/empathy-in-the-workplace-a-tool-for-effective-leadership/

Center for Creative Leadership Articles. (n.d.-c). *The irony of integrity.* Center for Creative Leadership. https://ccl.org/articles/white-papers/the-irony-of-integrity-a-study-of-the-character-strengths-of

Center for Creative Leadership Articles. (2017). *4 keys to strengthen your ability to influence others | CCL.* Center for Creative Leadership. https://www.ccl.org/articles/leading-effectively-articles/4-keys-strengthen-ability-influence-others/

Center for Creative Leadership Articles. (2018). *You can master the 3 ways to influence people.* Center for Creative Leadership. https://www.ccl.org/articles/leading-effectively-articles/three-ways-to-influence/

Center for Creative Leadership Blog. (2019, January 14). *What are the characteristics of a good leader?* Center for Creative Leadership. https://www.ccl.org/blog/characteristics-good-leader/

Cherry, K. (2014, June 25). *Situational theory of leadership.* Verywell Mind; Verywellmind. https://www.verywellmind.com/what-is-the-situational-theory-of-leadership-2795321

Cherry, K., & Morin, A. (2019). *How to become a stronger and more effective leader.* Verywell Mind. https://www.verywellmind.com/ways-to-become-a-better-leader-2795324

Cone, T. (2020, January 9). *What is innovation leadership?* Medium. https://medium.com/lightshed/what-is-innovation-leadership-8094f79620ca

Daskal, L. (2016, July 5). *Why the empathetic leader is the best leader - Lolly Daskal | leadership.* Lolly Daskal. https://www.lollydaskal.com/leadership/whats-empathy-got-leadership/

Downard, B. (2018, May 18). *101 Best leadership skills, traits & qualities - the complete list.* Brian Downard. https://briandownard.com/leadership-skills-list/

Doyle, L. (2019, March 7). *Leadership styles: 5 common approaches & how to find your own.* Northeastern University Graduate Programs. https://www.northeastern.edu/graduate/blog/leadership-styles/

Economy, P. (2015a, May 22). *7 Powerful habits for establishing credibility as a leader.* Inc.Com; Inc.

https://www.inc.com/peter-economy/8-powerful-habits-to-establish-credibility-as-a-leader.html

Economy, P. (2015b, August 27). *27 Powerful quotes to bring out the real greatness in you.* Inc.Com. https://www.inc.com/peter-economy/27-powerful-quotes-to-bring-out-the-real-greatness-in-you.html

Ellevate. (2019, October 10). *Five combination traits of an effective leader.* Forbes. https://www.forbes.com/sites/ellevate/2019/10/10/five-combination-traits-of-an-effective-leader/#73fadf0654ad

Ewing, T. (2020, August 11). *7 Things mentally tough people never do—based on science.* Forbes. https://www.forbes.com/sites/tonyewing/2020/08/11/7-things-mentally-tough-people-never-do-based-on-science/

Forbes. (2020). *America's most innovative leaders.* Forbes. https://www.forbes.com/lists/innovative-leaders/#28c02f7b26aa

Furnham, A. (2010). The Machiavellian Leader. *The elephant in the boardroom,* 140–151. https://doi.org/10.1057/9780230281226_6

Future of Working The Leadership and Career Blog. (2018, September 4). *12 Advantages and disadvantages of dictatorial leadership styles.* FutureofWorking.Com. https://futureofworking.com/12-advantages-and-disadvantages-of-dictatorial-leadership-styles/

Gallup Inc. (2019). *How Millennials want to work and live.* Gallup.Com. https://www.gallup.com/workplace/238073/millennials-work-live.aspx

Garnett, L. (2015, August 26). *7 Steps to go from an ordinary to extraordinary leader.* Inc.Com.

https://www.inc.com/laura-garnett/7-steps-to-go-from-ordinary-to-an-extraordinary-leader.html

Gifford, G. (2012, February 6). *Five keys to managing an unpredictable boss.* PrimeGenesis. https://www.primegenesis.com/our-blog/2012/02/five-keys-to-managing-an-unpredictable-boss-2/

Glassdoor Team. (2013, November 13). *Employers to retain half of their employees longer if bosses showed more appreciation; glassdoor survey.* US | Glassdoor for Employers. https://www.glassdoor.com/employers/blog/employers-to-retain-half-of-their-employees-longer-if-bosses-showed-more-appreciation-glassdoor-survey/

Half, R. (2018, November 7). *Effective employee retention strategies.* Roberthalf.Com. https://www.roberthalf.com/blog/management-tips/effective-employee-retention-strategies

Hasan, S. (2018, March 19). *Top 10 leadership qualities that make good leaders.* TaskQue. https://blog.taskque.com/characteristics-good-leaders/

Heathfield, S. M. (2004, October 9). *Leadership vision.* The Balance Careers; The Balance. https://www.thebalancecareers.com/leadership-vision-1918616

Hedges, K. (2018, October 25). *Don't have A leadership vision? Here's where to find it.* Forbes. https://www.forbes.com/sites/work-in-progress/2018/10/25/dont-have-a-leadership-vision-heres-where-to-find-it/#4787029da0a8

Inzlicht, M., Bartholow, B. D., & Hirsh, J. B. (2015). Emotional foundations of cognitive control. *Trends in Cognitive Sciences, 19*(3), 126–132. https://doi.org/10.1016/j.tics.2015.01.004

Jackowska, M., Brown, J., Ronaldson, A., & Steptoe, A. (2016). The impact of a brief gratitude intervention on subjective well-being, biology and sleep. *Journal of Health Psychology*, *21*(10), 2207–2217. https://doi.org/10.1177/1359105315572455

Jacobson, S. (2019, July 26). *Teamwork: Respecting others*. The Conover Company. https://www.conovercompany.com/teamwork-respecting-others/

Kankousky, M. (2017, October 17). *7 strategies to boost your leadership skills through self-awareness*. Insperity. https://www.insperity.com/blog/self-awareness/

Kenny, H. (2017, February 27). *Are you an unpredictable leader? –Leading from the deep end*. Leading from the Deep End. https://leadingfromthedeepend.com/are-you-an-unpredictable-leader/

Koch, A. (2019, March 20). *5 Things employees really want in a boss*. Business.Com. https://www.business.com/articles/what-employees-want-from-leaders/

Kruse, K. (2018, May 18). 5 Things all employees want from their leaders. *Forbes*. https://www.forbes.com/sites/kevinkruse/2018/05/16/5-things-all-employees-want-from-their-leaders/

Kyocera Contributor, & Reaume, A. (2018, November 5). *Kyocera BrandVoice: What workplace decision-makers can learn from Lean manufacturing techniques*. Forbes. https://www.forbes.com/sites/kyocera/2018/11/05/what-workplace-decision-makers-can-learn-from-lean-manufacturing-techniques/

Lenkic, P. (2017, August 15). *Unpredictable leadership is dangerous, not disruptive*. SmartCompany. https://www.smartcompany.com.au/people-human-resources/leadership/unpredictable-leadership-dangerous-not-disruptive/

Llopis, G. (2013, November 27). *The 4 most effective ways leaders solve problems.* Forbes. https://www.forbes.com/sites/glennllopis/2013/11/04/the-4-most-effective-ways-leaders-solve-problems/

Lucas, S. (2020, May 1). *What do employees want most from their managers?* The Balance Careers. https://www.thebalancecareers.com/what-employees-most-want-from-their-bosses-4117080

Malsam, W. (2019, June 4). *Top down vs. bottom up management: What's the difference?* ProjectManager.Com. https://www.projectmanager.com/blog/top-down-vs-bottom-up-management

Maxwell, J. C. (2000). *The 21 irrefutable laws of leadership : follow them and people will follow you.* Struik Christian Books. (Original work published 1998)

Maxwell, J. C. (2010). *Everyone communicates few connect : what the most effective people do differently.* Jaico.

Myatt, M. (2015, December 13). *5 Keys of dealing with workplace conflict.* Forbes. https://www.forbes.com/sites/mikemyatt/2012/02/22/5-keys-to-dealing-with-workplace-conflict/

Oxford English Online. (2020). *Soft skills.* Oxford English Online.

Patel, D. (2017, March 23). 11 Powerful traits of successful leaders. *Forbes.* https://www.forbes.com/sites/deeppatel/2017/03/22/11-powerful-traits-of-successful-leaders/

Patel, D. (2019). *14 Proven ways to improve your communication skills.* Entrepreneur. https://www.entrepreneur.com/article/300466

Porter, J. (2014, October 6). *You're more biased than you think.* Fast Company. https://www.fastcompany.com/3036627/youre-more-biased-than-you-think

Porter, S. H. (2018, January 11). *Council post: You win or you learn: Risk-Taking for leaders.* Forbes. https://www.forbes.com/sites/forbescoachescouncil/2018/01/11/you-win-or-you-learn-risk-taking-for-leaders/

Qin, X., Huang, M., Johnson, R. E., Hu, Q., & Ju, D. (2018). *The short-lived benefits of abusive supervisory behavior for actors: An investigation of recovery and work engagement.* Academy of Management Journal, 61(5), 1951–1975. https://doi.org/10.5465/amj.2016.1325

Qualtrics. (2018, November 2). *10 Powerful quotes on leadership for your organization.* Qualtrics. https://www.qualtrics.com/blog/10-powerful-leadership-quotes/

Reynolds, J. (2018). *10 Leadership qualities to look for when hiring a manager.* Tinypulse.Com. https://www.tinypulse.com/blog/leadership-qualities-when-hiring-a-manager

Savas, O. (2019). *Impact of dysfunctional leadership on organizational performance.* Global Journal of Management and Business Research, 37–41. https://doi.org/10.34257/gjmbravol19is1pg37

Schaeffer, B. (2018, December 1). *Machiavellian leadership: how toxicity can lead to an organization's demise.* Www.Firehouse.Com. https://www.firehouse.com/leadership/article/2102151

31/machiavellian-leadership-how-toxicity-can-lead-to-an-organizations-demise

Simons, P., Benders, J., Bergs, J., Marneffe, W., & Vandijck, D. (2016). *Has Lean improved organizational decision making?* International Journal of Health Care Quality Assurance, 29(5), 536–549. https://doi.org/10.1108/ijhcqa-09-2015-0118

Simplilearn. (2017, October 9). *Qualities of great leaders and great managers.* Simplilearn.Com; Simplilearn. https://www.simplilearn.com/leaders-and-managers-qualities-article

Singh, M. (2018, December 6). *Learning agility: How to measure it?* Mettl. https://blog.mettl.com/how-to-measure-individual-and-organizational-learning-agility/

Smarp Blog. (2020, August 6). *What are the top leadership skills that make a great leader?* Blog.Smarp.Com. https://blog.smarp.com/what-are-the-top-leadership-skills-that-make-a-great-leader

Smuin, A. (2017, July 13). *10 leadership skills every manager needs to succeed.* The CEO Magazine. https://theceomagazine.com/business/management-leadership/10-leadership-skills-every-manager-needs

SpriggHR. (2020a, January 8). *12 Essential leadership qualities • SpriggHR.* SpriggHR. https://www.sprigghr.com/blog/management-tips/12-essential-leadership-qualities/

SpriggHR. (2020b, January 13). *5 actionable employee retention strategies • SpriggHR.* SpriggHR. https://sprigghr.com/blog/management-tips/5-actionable-employee-retention-strategies/

Tech Support. (2013, October 17). *Problem solving ability*. The Complete Leader. https://thecompleteleader.org/problem-solving-ability

The Greenleaf Center for Servant Leadership. (2016). *What is servant leadership? - Greenleaf Center for Servant Leadership*. Greenleaf Center for Servant Leadership. https://www.greenleaf.org/what-is-servant-leadership/

Toffler, A. (1970). *Future shock*. Pan Books.

Tucker, R. B. (2017, February 10). *Six innovation leadership skills everybody needs to master*. Forbes. https://www.forbes.com/sites/robertbtucker/2017/02/09/six-innovation-leadership-skills-everybody-needs-to-master/

Walden University Blog. (n.d.). *What makes A good leader ten essential qualities to learn*. Www.Waldenu.Edu. https://www.waldenu.edu/programs/business/resource/what-makes-a-good-leader-ten-essential-qualities-to-learn

Wilbanks, C. H. (2018, August 22). *5 Ways to lead by serving*. The Wilbanks Consulting Group. https://www.wilbanksconsulting.com/blog/2018/8/22/5-ways-to-lead-by-serving

Wilson, A. G. (2015, March 26). *10 Most important leadership skills for team success*. ESkill. https://www.eskill.com/blog/important-leadership-skills-for-team-success/

Yaffe, P. (2011). *The 7% rule*. Ubiquity, 2011 (October), 1–5. https://doi.org/10.1145/2043155.2043156

Young Entrepreneur Council. (n.d.). *12 Employee Qualities That Managers Love*. The Muse. https://www.themuse.com/advice/12-ways-to-stand-out-to-your-boss-and-get-all-the-good-assignments-fun-projects-and-big-promotions

Zhu, J., & Zhang, B. (2019). *The double-edged sword effect of abusive supervision on subordinates' innovative behavior.* Frontiers in Psychology, 10. https://doi.org/10.3389/fpsyg.2019.00066

www.ingramcontent.com/pod-product-compliance
Lightning Source LLC
Chambersburg PA
CBHW071704210326
41597CB00017B/2333